MW01602837

THE CONTRIBUTION OF MONASTIC LIFE TO THE CHURCH AND THE WORLD

THE CONTRIBUTION OF MONASTIC LIFE TO THE CHURCH AND THE WORLD

Essays in Celebration of the Fiftieth Anniversary of Mount Saviour Monastery

Edited by

Martin Boler

and

Anthony J. Cernera

SACRED HEART UNIVERSITY PRESS
FAIRFIELD, CONNECTICUT

THE CONTRIBUTION OF MONASTIC LIFE TO THE CHURCH AND THE WORLD

*Essays in Celebration of the Fiftieth Anniversary
of Mount Saviour Monastery*

Edited by Martin Boler and Anthony J. Cernera

ISBN 1-888112-12-3 (hardcover)

Copyright 2006 by the Sacred Heart University Press

Contents

Illustrations follow page 92

Preface

MARTIN BOLER

The kingdom of heaven is like a treasure buried in a field which a person finds and hides again, and out of joy goes and sells all he has and buys that field. (Matthew 13:44)

As we celebrate the fiftieth anniversary of Mount Saviour Monastery, and as we read this passage from Matthew's Gospel, probably nothing better describes the situation of Fathers Damasus, Gregory, Placid, and Bernard when they founded Mount Saviour in the fields of the Hofbauer farm—joy. They experienced true joy which prompted all that followed. Their joy was the joy of the Paschal Lord which he wishes to share with us: "That my joy may be in you and your joy may be complete" (John 15:11).

One of the Psalms observes that seventy years is our allotted life span, and eighty for those who are strong. In the experience of our Founders and our subsequent experience, there has been an amount of emptiness and pain, but such has certainly not been the majority of our experience. Underlying our human angst, the Paschal joy of the Lord, with its source in the *agape* of the Father has been and is the underlying theme of our common life. It is our hope that in these pages something of the joy of the Lord may be evident in what is said of Mount Saviour as well as in the accounts of Benedictine life in general. Monasteries may be autonomous but our shared vision and interrelatedness is real.

We are especially grateful at this time for those who presented the papers on the occasion of our fiftieth anniversary included in this volume and who spent some time with the community telling us about their life and work. Some lectures originally presented on that occasion are not included here at the speaker's request and others included here were given on a different occasion. They all pertain to the theme of "The Contribution of Monastic Life to the Church and the World."

A special word of thanks is due to Anthony J. Cernera, president of Sacred Heart University, for his constant support and friendship, and for his invaluable assistance in editing and publishing these essays through Sacred Heart University Press.

The monks of Mount Saviour, our Oblates, and our friends are grateful for our first fifty years, and honored that we can share with you a small measure of our joy. May all who read these words grow closer to our crucified and risen Lord and to each other in His service.

The Meaning and Purpose
of this Benedictine Moment

JEROME KODELL

As I contemplate the path of Benedictine monasticism in coming years, I recall two wonderful stories from the Desert monks of the fourth century. The first is a story about Abba Agathon:

> Going to town one day to sell some small articles, Abba Agathon met a cripple on the roadside, who asked him to carry him to town. He did so. When they arrived, the cripple said, "Put me down where you sell your goods." He did so. When Abba Agathon had sold an article, the cripple said, "Buy me a cake." He did so. Every time he sold something, the cripple would ask him to buy something else. He did so. When he had sold everything, the cripple said, "Would you carry me back and put me down where you found me?" He did so. Then the cripple said, "Agathon, you are filled with divine blessings in heaven and on earth." Raising his eyes, Agathon saw no man; it was the angel of the Lord.

I visualize monastics of the twenty-first century in the person of Abba Agathon, ready to be used for the good of the world, represented by the crippled beggar (who is really Christ). We will have many calls on us because of the gift we have received from God. We will not always be able to evaluate the requests thoroughly, but except in obviously inappropriate situations we will try to answer them for the good of the Church and the world. We will have to listen very deeply because those who request, even those in authority in the Church, will not always know what they are asking. We will learn to listen then, as now, only through prayer.

The second story is about Abba Joseph, who was asked about prayer:

> Abba Lot went to see Abba Joseph and said to him, "Abba, as far as I can, I say my little office, I fast a little, I pray and meditate, I live in peace as far as I can, I purify my thoughts. What else can I do?" Then the old man stood up and stretched his hands toward heaven. His fingers became like ten lamps of fire and he said to him, "If you will, you can become all flame."

In the past century and a half, the Church needed us to aid its missionary work in the building years. We have already begun our work for the coming time, which will be to help people enter deeply into the mystery of God, especially through contemplative prayer. We must pray to become flame so that we may warm and illuminate our brothers and sisters, and help them to become flame.

At the present time, Benedictine monasticism is still in the wake of the renewal of Vatican II. The mandate to return to the sources has inaugurated a very fruitful time for us. Probably there has been more widespread search into the history and meaning of monasticism in the past thirty years than at any other time. We have learned much and are still learning.

This era was preceded by the final stage of the nineteenth-century European monastic revival, which had come out of the ashes of the French Revolution and secularization movements, and was born in the Romantic age. It was translated to this hemisphere and adapted to the local cultures. Most of our communities and many of us were part of that. The mixture of influences and theories animating that revival caused monastic life in this hemisphere in some cases to grow like Topsy. Especially in the United States, Benedictines were parochialized like other religious orders. That has been our recent point of departure.

Before all of that, a movement that had nothing particularly to do with monasticism has had a pervasive influence on monasticism up to the present time. This was the Enlightenment, the Age of

Reason, the exaltation of the intellect. This movement has done much good and should not be made a whipping post for all current problems. But we must say that because of the Enlightenment it is very hard for us to understand key aspects of monastic spirituality from the earlier ages, especially *lectio divina* and prayer. That is changing and will have to change for the coming age.

Western civilization is now in a period of integrating emotion and intellect, feelings and reason, right brain and left brain. Monasticism has already reaped much from this movement and in this area is beginning to contribute much to Western spirituality. Simply put, I believe that in the West the enlightenment of the intellect of the eighteenth century is finally being followed in spirituality by an enlightenment of the heart for the twenty-first century, in which monastics will have an important role to play.

Monasticism in Our World

Benedictine monasticism is still a curiosity in the world, even in the Church, and even in various degrees for other religious orders. A story Abbot Patrick Barry tells is indicative. He was out walking at Ampleforth when a group of tourists approached him and asked if this was really an Abbey. He said, yes it is. Well, they asked, where are the ruins?

Recently this attitude has been changing, at least to the extent that monasticism, though still a curiosity, is more and more an attractive curiosity because of a growing hunger for a deeper life. Seekers of transcendence are coming from various religious faiths and from no identified faith. There is increased interest in retreats, silence, prayer, the spiritual journey, books about monasteries and Benedictine spirituality. More and more people are affiliating as oblates. Monasteries have historically served an ecumenical role and this is growing again today. Monasteries are by nature non-threatening environments, where questioners and seekers of all kinds, believers and non-believers, can come without making a statement about themselves or revealing their own faith stance.

This interest is true no less of Catholics than others, but there is also confusion in the Church. Diocesan structures do not know where monasticism fits, especially now that the parochial work force is drying up. This is true of all religious life as such. Recently the Dominicans were invited out of the Atlanta archdiocese because there was no immediate need for them in diocesan ministries. There was no recognition of the gift of their life and charism for the Church independent of covering assignments. Some, of course, do understand. The late Bishop Albert L. Fletcher of my own Diocese of Little Rock invited the Discalced Carmelite Sisters to found a cloistered monastery in 1950 for the benefit of their life of prayer to the local church, but had to weather complaints about their "non-productivity" in the ministry. The laity understands sisters and priests as parochial workers, but not brothers, even the Christian Brothers. Why don't they go all the way and get ordained?

Similarly, contemporary Church authority has a hard time categorizing an institution from the early Church within the current structure. In men's monasteries, the restriction of abbatial leadership to the ordained (because of more recent canonical norms) is already hampering many smaller communities and some larger ones, as since Vatican II more and more of the potential leaders are not being ordained.

Relating to Other Orders

There are many different patterns in the relationship of monasticism to other religious orders. We have generally had little structural relationship with other religious because the organization in provinces is so different from a loose collection of autonomous monasteries. The clarification of our identity mandated by Vatican II may be differentiating us in a substantial way even more, but I think something is percolating which will bring us into a new relationship in the years ahead. I want to share with you my own experience in this area since becoming abbot, which possibly sheds an interesting light on a new role the Church may be asking of us.

Immediately on becoming abbot in 1989 I began receiving mailings from the Conference of Major Superiors of Men. I had heard that though CMSM had been founded with strong Benedictine involvement (and the first president had been an abbot), participation by Benedictines was by now minimal. (It is my impression that women Benedictines, at least in the U.S., have been more active in the Leadership Conference of Women Religious [LCWR].) I have been told that one reason for the abbots' absence was that at a particular juncture in the early 1970s it became the common wisdom to blame monastic influences for the problems in active orders. Abbots got tired of hearing this. Whether or not this was a factor, what I feel has been far more influential on the abbots' absence, then and now, is that CMSM is designed for active orders organized in the provincial system, with programs that offer little that is particularly helpful to monastic superiors. We monastics have our own workshops and meetings; besides, the dues and the costs of meetings are high, and they are extras for our already strained budgets.

One major exception among the abbots in 1989 was Abbot James Jones of Conception, who was on CMSM's national board. At his urging, I agreed to show some interest, and I went in 1992 to a national meeting in San Antonio. I was surprised by the warmth and special attention with which I was greeted.

Apparently on the strength of that participation, several months later I was invited to be a representative at an Inter-American Assembly of Religious in Santo Domingo, where again I was treated with the utmost attentiveness. I was struck that out of all the delegates representing religious life in the western hemisphere, forty from Canada, fifty from the U.S., and forty-five from Latin America, only two of us, Sister Cecilia Dwyer of Bristow and myself, represented any monastic order. (Archbishop Rembert Weakland was also there, but as a speaker). There were no Benedictines from Canada and all of Latin America, and no Cistercians, Camaldolese, or Carmelites, male or female, from the whole hemisphere. But it became fairly clear to me that we were not so much excluded as unavailable. A major meeting of religious life was convoked for our hemisphere, and monastics were almost unrepresented. This was not potentially so much a loss to monasticism as to the Church and to the future of religious life as a whole in this part of the world.

Several months later I received another call from CMSM: Would I be a member of the Justice and Peace Committee? This floored me, since though justice and peace are high on my list, I have no special visibility in that arena. I mentioned this and was told that CMSM was trying actively to incorporate the contemplative or monastic dimension into its work, and this committee was by definition the most activist. All they wanted me there for was as a monastic presence, to participate in whatever way I could.

All this has made a big impression on me, and I take it as a sign of new possibilities for U.S. religious life in the immediate future. I am being invited not because of some personal achievement or record, but because I represent monastic life and I am available. This pattern has continued. I was asked to be on the planning committee for the 1998 joint meeting of CMSM and LCWR representing the monastic dimension and eventually to give presentations on contemplative prayer when a speaker could not be found from the more strictly contemplative orders. The new Council for the Study of Religious Life has asked me to be part of their program committee for the same reason, as a representative of the monastic dimension of religious life.

Leaders of the other orders have told me that they are aware of the common monastic roots of religious life and of the need to reawaken that dimension in their own congregations, but they need to look to monastics for help. I think we should listen carefully to discern if this is our call, not so much to help ourselves and our own in-house concerns—because the offerings of CMSM and LCWR are oriented to provincialate issues—but as a critical service of the Church in a time of reorganization and renewal of religious life. We have something that the larger world of religious life is asking us to share. I honestly do not know how best to share monasticism with other religious beyond being present and responding to the possibilities of the relationship under the Spirit's inspiration. As Jesus taught, "The gift you have received, give as a gift" (Matthew 10:8). I feel certain that as we share the gift of our life with other religious in a way we cannot clearly foresee, we will receive from them a gift we cannot yet expect.

Icon of Transfiguration

In 1996 Pope John Paul II issued *Vita Consecrata,* an apostolic exhortation meant to be the guiding document on religious life for some years. Without fanfare, the pope moved away from the traditional biblical image for the religious life, the rich young man of the Synoptic Gospels (which he had adopted for his earlier reflection on the religious life in *Redemptionis Donum,* in 1984). Instead he used another pivotal Synoptic scene, the Transfiguration, calling attention to the "icon of the transfigured Christ."

The rich young man story has never been satisfactory as an image for the religious life, because the primary challenge of the story is applicable to all Christians, not just religious: leave everything and follow Christ. The early Church saw it that way, to judge from Clement of Alexandria's famous sermon, in which the rich man who will be saved is anyone who responds to the call of Christ by repentance. The icon of the Transfiguration is much better because at the same time it protects the unity of the Christian vocation in all its manifestations and also allows for the uniqueness of the religious vocation. For our interest here, it also makes an important connection with the monastic tradition.

On one hand, *Vita Consecrata* reflects Vatican II's doctrine of the universal call to holiness:

> All those reborn in Christ are called to live out with the strength which is the Spirit's gift the chastity appropriate to their state in life, obedience to God and to the Church, and a reasonable detachment from material possessions: for all are called to holiness which consists in the perfection of love. (30)

But the document also recognizes a uniqueness to the vocation to the religious or consecrated life:

> All are equally called to follow Christ, to discover in him the ultimate meaning of their lives. . . . But those who are called to the consecrated life have a special experience of the light which shines forth from the incarnate Word. (*VC* 15)

The Pope locates vocation in the special religious experience of those called to the consecrated life. "Religious experience" rather than "call" becomes the common denominator for all radical Christian vocations, including but not only the religious life. The desire to follow Christ more closely springs from an experience of God evoking a response that leads by God's design to various expressions: the consecrated life, lay single life, Christian marriage, priesthood or other ministry. Not all Christians respond to these experiences, but for those who do, this is the real call to commit radically to the kingdom.

The best translation of the eunuch passage in Matthew 19, which is a source for the vocation to consecrated chastity and therefore for religious life, is that some followers of Christ become eunuchs not "*for the sake of* the kingdom" (that is, with a purpose in mind) but "*because of* the kingdom" (that is, being overwhelmed by an experience of the kingdom that drives them to live in a way they had not planned on). Their lives explode and no longer fit into customary patterns. The uniqueness of this vocation within the Christian vocation is expressed by the profession of vows, in which the personal and initially private response to the experience of the kingdom is brought into public view for the sake of Church and world:

> This profession . . . makes them a kind of sign and pro-
> phetic statement for their community and for the world;
> consequently they can echo in a particular way the ecstatic
> words spoken by Peter: "Lord, it is well that we are here
> . . ." How good for us to be with you, to devote ourselves
> to you, to make you the one focus of our lives! (*VC* 15)

They are dedicated to Christ "professionally"—by public profession—and are no longer completely private figures in the Church, even though the essence of their profession may be lived secretly.

The Transfiguration is particularly appropriate as the icon for a radical and transforming response to God's call because it was a momentous event for the three apostles, but even more because it is treated as a key religious event in Jesus' own life. It is presented as the occasion when Jesus comprehended fully the cost and the glory of his mission and embraced it. Luke's account makes this especially graphic. The inner experience of Jesus affects his countenance: "While he was praying, his face changed in *appearance* and his clothes became dazzling white" (Luke 9:29). At his baptism, the voice from heaven told Jesus, "You are my beloved Son; with you I am well pleased" (Luke 3:22). But after Jesus has realized the true nature and the cost of his vocation and embraced it, the voice speaks to the disciples: "This is my chosen Son; listen to him" (9:35). As the result of this definitive vocation experience, Jesus can be presented as the teacher of salvation.

The icon of the Transfiguration is an image both of the response to divine vocation and of transformation in the presence of God. It connects with the experience of Moses on Sinai.

> As Moses came down from Mount Sinai with the two tablets of the commandments in his hands, he did not know that the skin of his face had become radiant while he conversed with the Lord. (Exodus 34:29)

St. Paul makes this experience of Moses the pattern of all who fix their gaze on God:

> All of us, gazing with unveiled faces on the glory of the Lord, are being transformed from glory to glory as from the Lord who is the Spirit. (2 Corinthians 3:18)

The icon of the Transfiguration as an image for the consecrated life, as I mentioned earlier, has a particular resonance for those of us in the monastic tradition. In Greek Orthodox monasticism, Tabor has been a symbol of the hesychastic search for God under the rubric of "prayer of the heart." Unlike some more intellectual strains which came west, the immediate aim of this prayer (especially by repetition of the name of Jesus) is to offer the heart directly to God. The struggle is more with inordinate desires than with distracting thoughts. The fruit of this prayer is the "Taboric light," the same that filled Jesus during his transfiguration.

Though it has roots in the teaching of the Desert monks, the great champion of this spirituality was Gregory Palamas, a Mount Athos monk and then archbishop of Thessalonica in the fourteenth century. Mysticism always leads one on a rocky road. His teaching was condemned in 1342, then approved five years later; ultimately it received the sanction of his canonization in 1368. Typical of the struggles that often accompany the debate about Taboric prayer was the nickname given to Gregory's followers by his enemies: *omphalopsychoi*, "those who have their souls in their navels."

Prayer

We have all been touched, moved, and changed personally by a transfiguration experience. That profound experience on the mountaintop once swept us off our feet and impelled us to this vocation and our monastic way of life. However, we know the statistics on the religious and priests who have left this calling and turned to other ways of life. Each of us knows many stories of those who have made that decision, and we know that often it was the right decision. But we must also realize that sometimes the icon of the transfiguration was allowed to dim and die in the lives of those validly called and initially committed.

We also know religious who, though they have remained in their communities, have ceased to live out of the experience that inspired their commitment. They are distinguished by the attitudes identified already by Cassian as the great enemies of the spiritual life, the passions of anger and sadness. These are tragic figures who have forgotten that the source of their joy is within them and have doomed themselves to casting about futilely for meaning and satisfaction. Sadly they have somehow lost contact with the wellspring of their vocation.

The eminent theologian Karl Rahner produced volumes and volumes of commentary on God, redemption, the life of grace. Scattered throughout the tomes of long and often convoluted sentences are short and clear statements recognized as seminal insights that continue to be much quoted. One of those statements bears on our subject here: "The Christian of the future will be a mystic or will not exist at all."[1] By mysticism, Rahner explains, he does not mean some esoteric phenomenon but "a genuine experience of God emerging from the very heart of our existence." He goes on to comment that the source of spiritual conviction comes not from theology but from the personal experience of God. This statement, made late in Rahner's career, is similar to the comment reported of Thomas Aquinas at the end of his life about his volumes of theology being so much straw.

If monasticism is to mean anything and be of any value in the coming age, it will be within this context of the living experience of God. I think we could paraphrase Rahner to say "Monastics will be rooted in contemplative prayer or they will not exist at all." What is different about this from the present or the recent past? The difference is not that true monastics have not failed to be people of contemplative prayer up to now, in the sense of a vibrant personal relationship with God beyond words. But wherever monasticism is enmeshed in a modern or postmodern culture of mechanization, instant communication, and unlimited information (in other words, for practically all our monasteries), the external structures and rhythm no longer lead naturally to a contemplative existence, as they could in a more enclosed, less invaded environment where the main work rhythm was manual agriculture. A deep experience of God, constantly renewed, will be necessary to offset the threats to faith from a defiantly secular and even atheistic culture. What is already true today will continue to be the norm in the future: only monastics committed to an intense personal prayer life beyond the communal structures will find the joy and transformation that this life offers.

A desert elder compared the pursuit of God to a dog with the taste of the hare in its mouth: "A monk should observe the dogs on the hunt for hares. Only the one who has seen the hare chases it, while the others that have seen the dog run after him, but only so long as they don't get tired." Only the dog that has seen the hare will keep up the long chase while the hare is out of sight. He will be stopped "neither by chasms, forests, nor thickets, neither by scratching, thorns, or wounds." A monastic may go to choir because it is a community observance. But this alone will not sustain one through the thicket of daily life. Only daily focus on the Lord in personal prayer, constant "sighting of the hare," will provide the necessary strength.

This may sound self-evident but it is not. Speaking from my own experience, when I entered the monastery I expected the rhythm of prayer and work, scheduled community prayer and work done in obedience, to carry me to happiness and sainthood. The "prayer" in the Benedictine motto *ora et labora* was understood to be the Liturgy of the Hours. There was also "mental prayer," which was hard to distinguish from discursive meditation. The recovery of *lectio divina* as the third "l"—liturgy, labor, *lectio*—is a recent phenomenon, and even this has often been understood more in the direction of study than of personal prayer. We have lived with the unspoken expectation that one's personal prayer life would emerge naturally within the system. We have not seen a focus on training in contemplative prayer, under whatever form or method, as critical to monastic formation and monastic life. But it will be essential from now on.

For monasticism is and always will be a life of prayer, but not in the limited sense common in our culture, where a life of prayer is comprehensible only as a chain of prayer actions of the mind, sometimes involving the body. One is "prayerful" in intervals; and the shorter the intervals the more prayerful you are. Monasticism bears witness to a different understanding of the spiritual world—to the possibility of being immersed continually in the mystery of God, living out of the transforming experience of God that changes everything.

To "pray always" does not mean, as we all know, to be in church or on your knees all the time. It is to be living continually under the dominion of God's reign making decisions moment to moment under that dominion more and more habitually and naturally as we grow in a life of prayer (what Newman calls "learning the language of heaven")—or better, as our lives merge with the current of prayer that is already in us by the divine indwelling. To reach that state we do need regular times of prayer, but not prayers to substitute for prayer. The Hours of the *Opus Dei* are anchors and reminders in the daily journey. "Nothing is to be preferred to the Work of God" in order to establish our commitment to the priority of God's dominion, but only within a vibrant framework of personal prayer will the Hours of the Office be enough to sustain the prayer life necessary for the coming age. For this, each monastic must faithfully and without fail come before God for a time every day in absolute inner stillness, availability and vulnerability. Only this kind of giving up control, a blind and helpless act of trust, without words, images, or our own insights and plans, will develop in us the radical faith by which we can give Church and world our monastic gift.

Monasticism sinks its roots into the real world of God by seeking an ever deeper union with God in prayer. This vocation is a ministry of prayer by which a community makes itself available to God as a channel of grace for Christ's saving mission in this world.

I have been profoundly affected by a statement of Archbishop Desmond Tutu in a sermon he preached in 1984 in Washington, D.C. He thanked Christians around the world for the help that had come to South Africa through their prayer. But he was not making the usual connection about prayers for a particular intention: he was not thanking us for including his suffering people in our prayer intentions. In short, Archbishop Tutu was not thanking us for remembering his people in prayer, but just for *praying*, for God in unseen ways uses the availability of our hearts to heal other hearts and other situations around the world.

This is an insight from the ancient Christian tradition of prayer, which understands the deeper connections beyond request and response. Though not all prayer is petitionary, because of the mystery of the Incarnation all prayer is intercessory; the divine pattern is for human beings to be channels of grace to one another.

Monasticism focuses and concretizes this insight for the Church. Our call is to become channels of blessing for the world by making ourselves more and more available for God's action in and through us. Through the humility of deep prayer we are able to penetrate beyond the false self to our true center, where God is always waiting. We prostrate ourselves interiorly, offering ourselves to God for the world. And God distributes gifts in our name, without our ever knowing where or how. Thomas Merton said: "In the economy of God's grace you may be sharing his gifts with someone you will never know until you get to heaven."

Periods of vitality in monastic history have not always been times of clearest focus. The nineteenth-century renewal had great vitality, producing an amazing Benedictine expansion up to Vatican II, but at the same time considerable confusion about the role and purpose of monasticism. Now we are in a time of focus, driven by the mandate to religious orders of Vatican II, and possibly sharpened by the drop in numbers. In the coming age, this renewal of focus will drive us to greater clarity about personal prayer in the monastic mission to the world and in the holiness and wholeness of monastics. We still have to interiorize the insight of monastic tradition expressed in *The Cloud of Unknowing*:

> One loving, blind desire for God alone is more valuable in itself, more pleasing to God and to the saints, more beneficial to your own growth, and more helpful to your friends, both living and dead, than anything else you could do.[2]

As a religious superior, I must know that the most important work I do for my community on any day takes place in my time of silence in the presence of God.

Lectio Divina

I mentioned earlier that because of the pervasive effects of the Enlightenment it is difficult for us to grasp the original concept of *lectio divina*, though the recovery of this tradition since Vatican II has had wonderful effects in monasticism and the larger Church. The pope's letter (July 7, 1999) looking ahead to the fifteen-hundredth anniversary of the founding of Subiaco (and therefore Benedictine monasticism) contained a ringing endorsement and appreciation of our tradition of *lectio*. If you are like me, these compliments about Benedictine *lectio* make you squirm. We are not as sure as we used to be about what we are supposed to do in *lectio*. It used to be simple, but some of the writing since Vatican II has made it complicated.

There are authors dealing very beautifully and I think correctly with *lectio* and their impact may eventually be great. But my experience is that the word *lectio* in *lectio divina* has more misled than helped us. Several times in the past few years I have had monastics rather far along on the spiritual path express anxiety over not being able to concentrate on "reading" in their time set for *lectio*. They know that *lectio* means reading and they only know reading in the modern aggressive sense. They feel guilty when drawn to silence.

This is because they think of *lectio* as "spiritual reading," a modern exercise that has its place as a preliminary or complement to *lectio*, but is more akin to study than to prayer. During the past year or so I reviewed two books on *lectio divina*. They had beautiful subtitles—"An Ancient Prayer That is Ever New"; "Praying the Bible"—but neither one of them got to the point. The prayer in the titles did not effectively make it to the text. They both left the impression that *lectio divina* is an intellectual exercise.

Guigo II's medieval synthesis of the *lectio* process in the ladder of *lectio*, *meditatio*, *oratio*, and *contemplatio* is well known, but our Western minds have focused on the first two steps, translating them simply into textual reading and discursive meditation, while practically ignoring *oratio* and treating *contemplatio* as a separate exercise. Until *lectio divina* is understood as a prayer method with contemplation as its goal, its power for transformation will not be released among us.

Those who cannot let go of the text are in the same situation as spiritual seekers who stall on the road of prayer because they cannot let go of words. In both cases the practitioners will fill their heads but not necessarily their hearts. Because of the deep scripture background monastics contain in their minds and hearts after years of the Divine Office and other exposures to the word of God, we do not need literally to read anything in order to practice *lectio divina*. Some days, or maybe most days as this life goes on, we go directly to *contemplatio*. Meanwhile the old familiar and simple method of poring over a familiar biblical text—a psalm, a Mass reading—savoring the words and phrases, "seeking the heart of God in the word of God" (Gregory the Great) without pressure to move or finish or know anything at the end, is still one of the best ways to do *lectio*. Recently, Cambridge professor Eamonn Duffy referred insightfully to *lectio* as "slow brooding over the tradition." In my Arkansas way of understanding it, *lectio divina* does not mean becoming a great exegete but in becoming familiar enough and at home enough with the word of God that it will let you turn it over and scratch its belly.

Monasticism and the World

The monastery, like the Church, exists not for itself but for the world. However, the monastic and the Christian have to *be* themselves before they can be of service to the world. A discussion of prayer and *lectio divina* is logically prior to the question of what monastics do for the world. We have already stressed that through our prayer itself the world outside the monastery is affected in profound ways that we can never trace. Our work also, as expression of our life of prayer, shares this effectiveness beyond our walls.

At the end of October I attended an international Benedictine education conference at Worth Abbey in England, along with the lay headmaster of our Academy and a monk teacher. The primary focus was on secondary education, but participants reflected a spectrum of Benedictine education efforts from kindergarten through the university.

The published schedule was strong and attractive, including Latin American and Asian representatives and a presentation on Newark Abbey's inner-city school that surprised our imaginations about how the Benedictine spirit and tradition can be transmitted in an increasingly secularized world as we pass to a new millennium.

With regard to the Third World, we were first of all surprised by the numbers. Benedictine schools in Europe and the U.S. are typically caring for students in the hundreds, but representatives from the Philippines, Chile, and Mexico are enrolling thousands. The total enrollment in the Philippines is about thirty thousand.

But what they are doing with these numbers of students is the point. All are involved in creative initiatives to transmit Benedictine spirituality to their students and faculty. The schools in Chile developed and operated by laity in the Manquehue movement, for example, have oratories where the Work of God is prayed together morning, noon, and evening; *lectio* groups are formed during school years which carry over for many graduates into adult *lectio* group sessions weekly. This spiritual formation undergirds an organized program of service in the local community, and regular *convivencias*, celebrations of friendship which include mutual accountability and discernment of fidelity.

The lay speakers proved by years of experience that Benedictine education is not dead, nor is the decline in the number of professed a sign of hopelessness, but that there are new possibilities many of us have not yet tapped. The impact of the meeting went far beyond Benedictine schools. We saw new possibilities for communicating the Benedictine gift we have been given, applicable in some way to practically every Benedictine community, if not in education, then in retreat work, hospitality, and local outreach.

One of our contemporary hazards is compartmentalization, being very serious about our spiritual quest but very hesitant to bring it openly into our equally serious professionalism in education, pastoral service, and even hospitality. People expect excellence in our service, but do not these days expect us to bring our search for God into it. For some reason we have become embarrassed about doing this. We must recover the ability to talk about the center and driving force of our life. This will affect not only our giving of the gift with which we have been entrusted, but our ability to attract others to this life.

Now that we are recovering the contemplative dimension of our life we must not automatically jettison all the ministries we have accumulated. This would be another compartmentalization. We seem to be on the threshold of a renewal of authentic Benedictine education, for example, and to disown it out of hand would be irresponsible.

In the Dominican tradition, preaching is *contemplata aliis tradere*, to pass on to others what we have learned by contemplation. This is certainly true of the Benedictine tradition as well. Contemplation here means not only a way of deep prayer but a whole attitude indicated by the opening word of the Rule, "Listen." This is why the *lectio* in *lectio divina* must not be limited rigidly to a written text. For Dominic and for us, the *contemplata* in *contemplata aliis tradere* includes potentially everything: gaining a divine perspective on reality. The poet George Herbert called prayer "the Christian plummet sounding heaven and earth."

The monk's place in the world and the right to speak to the world from a monastery was highlighted in letters Thomas

Merton exchanged with two prominent American theologians in the 1960s, in the heat of the struggle for civil rights and the canonization of the secular city as the arena for service. Merton had written "Letters to a White Liberal," in which he questioned the sincerity of the white liberal's commitment to reforms that would benefit blacks, saying it would go only as far as the white's self-interest. Martin Marty blasted him in a review: "How dare this escapist monk tell those of us who labor for justice in the cities that our work will fail?" Two-and-a-half years later, after the riots of 1967, Marty wrote an open letter to Merton apologizing for his review and admitting Merton's evaluation from the monastery had been accurate, while analyses closer to the scene had not.

Around the same time, Rosemary Ruether wrote Merton that monasticism involved a misunderstanding of the gospel, and that monks would do better to come out of their refuges and work for God's kingdom in the arena where the battles were being fought. Merton retorted, "Is there anything you can do in the city more effectively than I can do in the country, to stop the war in Vietnam?" There followed a substantive dialogue in which both compromised, he admitting there was a hands-on dimension of the struggle closed to him, and she grudgingly making room for the role of the contemplative.

The threat of escapism is a real and constant concern for monasticism. Our contemplation should make us more rather than less aware of the plight of the afflicted and the oppressed, of the struggle for human and civil rights. It enables us to see the world selflessly and opens within us what has been called a "contemplative wound," an inability to be satisfied or complacent while so much suffering and injustice exists. Monasteries are now, and must continue to be, places where justice and peace efforts find a home and support. In ways that were not open to Merton, most Benedictine communities are now able to combine an active outreach in peace and justice issues with a contemplative search for God.

Our inspiration for this commitment comes from the gospel, but it receives a special emphasis from the Rule in its insistence on the sacredness of every life, seeing Christ in each person. I think there is also an untapped resource in Benedict's concept of mutual obedience as a guide for human relations and even a more complete and rounded understanding of obedience in religious life and in the Church.

A Monastic Doctor of the Church

A recent development in the Church which may not have attracted the particular attention of monastics nevertheless has important significance for us. I refer to the naming of St. Therese of Lisieux as a Doctor of the Church. For one thing, though there have been many Doctors with monastic roots or spirituality, such as Basil, Jerome, Augustine, Peter Damian, Anselm, Bernard, and even her Carmelite colleagues Teresa and John of the Cross, Therese is the first Doctor since St. Bede in the eighth century to have spent her whole religious life in the cloister. The others typically had high-profile influence as bishops or Church reformers; their monasticism was incidental to their nomination.

Because of her public image, Therese's nomination seemed inappropriate at first. She is not associated with weighty doctrine nor a large body of literature (though she wrote more than John of the Cross) nor with the wisdom of age (having died at twenty-four). But closer examination bears out the wisdom of the choice, and the doctrine highlighted by the choice is highly monastic. St. Therese has been ill-served by early biographers who pictured her as a sweet (to the point of syrupy) and naive child preserved from the harsh realities of life. This was in fact how she began, but she broke from this mold thoroughly during her short years in the cloister. Now we know that she had to deal with great physical and mental suffering, and spent the last two years in a dark night which included temptations to atheism. Her importance for the modern search for God is indicated by her influence on Thomas Merton, who credited her significant role in his vocation, and on Dorothy Day, who wrote a biography of Therese. Neither of these two persons would be by any stretch be considered saccharine nor indifferent to the plight of the larger world.

I see the distinctive teaching of Therese deriving from, or supported by, her monastic vocation in two ways: in her "little way" of following Christ, and in her understanding of the missionary power of love. Her "little way" was an undramatic response of faith and love at every moment, striving for holiness by accepting sufferings and doing the smallest things with complete commitment to God's will even in the midst of her doubts, embracing everything that came as a sign of God's love and care. This is reminiscent of emphases in the *Rule of Benedict* that are making Benedictine spirituality so attractive beyond the monastery these days. Therese spoke of a "little way," Benedict of a "little rule."

Before Benedict's time people were discouraged by the impossibility of matching the heroic feats of the Desert generation, but Benedict put emphasis on doing the daily tasks well, small or large, without worrying about heroic observances. He also insisted on embracing the will of God as it comes in each moment. The great enemy on the road of holiness is murmuring, deadly because it is the denial of God's loving presence, a type of functional atheism.

This spiritual doctrine originates, of course, in the teaching of Jesus, but is hard to hold and tends to fade periodically before theories of spiritual elitism in one form or another. It is arguable that St. Francis de Sales, a primary influence on Therese, was named a Doctor of the Church largely for reopening the way of holiness to the laity four hundred years ago. But by the time of Vatican II we were back into first- and second-class roads to glory. The Council reiterated the universal call to holiness, and both Therese's little way and Benedict's little rule provide tools for a modern response. It is striking that Therese eventually gave up on the spiritual books of her time and drew her nourishment from a form of *lectio divina* of the gospels (at a time when Bible reading was not encouraged).

In 1927, two years after he had canonized her, Pope Pius XI declared St. Therese patron of all missionaries, men and women, and of all the missions throughout the world, joining her to St. Francis Xavier, who had already been named patron of the missions by Pope Pius X in 1904. This was a remarkable statement by the Church: an enclosed contemplative nun who spent all her nine years of religious life in the monastery was put on an equal footing as missionary patron with the Jesuit missionary who spent most of his religious life spreading the gospel in India and Japan.

As powerful a statement as this was about the effectiveness of a hidden life of prayer on Church and world, the message has still not come through crystal clear, even in our post-Vatican II age. Even in the current renewal of religious life there is controversy over mission and prayer, as witnessed in the findings of the Nygren-Ukeritis survey of religious in the U.S. in 1993. Perhaps this new recognition of St. Therese, patron of missionaries from within her monastery, can help move the Church to a deeper comprehension.

Many religious orders disappeared during the French Revolution and the accompanying secularization. Orders which could prove some social usefulness because of hospital or school work had a remote chance of survival; but contemplative orders, perceived as not only superstitious, but worse, socially useless, were closed universally. There were about fifteen hundred Benedictine and Cistercian monasteries in Europe in 1789; twenty years later only thirty or so remained. The same philosophy permeated the German secularization of the nineteenth century which figured in the history of many of our foundations.

Even though the Church continues to regenerate out of those ashes, the issue of the validity of a hidden contemplative life has never been adequately and finally validated. In the renewal days of the 1960s, serious challenges were raised even within the Church to the "luxury" of a hidden life of prayer when there were real needs to be met on the streets. We noticed that in the controversies surrounding Merton. The issue is still alive even in religious life. A diocesan hermit recently told of an exchange in a personal letter between religious that had been shared with him: "The Church should do away with hermits. . . . All they do is pray, anyway." But the recovery of and renewal since Vatican II of the older prayer tradition of the Church has been leading us to a deeper understanding in this area. I see the recognition at this time of St. Therese's teaching and her contemplative missionary role as a step in this direction.

The ideas of prayer and mission were certainly not contradictory for her. Even within the cloister St. Therese had a dream of being sent to the missionary scene of Vietnam, where there were two Carmelite monasteries. Her poor state of health made that impossible, and in the middle of a novena she came to understand that she could fulfill her missionary vocation another way. Her understanding of how her missionary vocation was to be exercised from within the monastery is expressed in a passage from her writings read in the Office for her feast:

> Love appeared to me to be the hinge for my vocation. Indeed I knew that the Church had a body composed of various members, but in this body the necessary and more noble member was not lacking; I knew that the Church had a heart and that such a heart appeared to be aflame with love. I knew that one love drove the members of the Church to action, that if this love were extinguished the apostles would have proclaimed the gospel no longer, the martyrs would have shed their blood no more.[3]

This is a very monastic insight. Divine love is the force powering the work of salvation in the world, and Therese's realization was to see that by letting that love be released through herself by the channel of her total availability to God through her life focused in contemplative prayer, she was reaching people far beyond the monastery and providing grace for the hands-on work of the missionaries. Hans von Balthasar said that Therese solved the debate about action and contemplation with her view of contemplation *as* action.

Most of our communities are far from being completely enclosed as Therese's was, so we serve the mission of the church in a hands-on way as well as in the secret time of prayer. But she reminds us that the active mission depends on the power of divine love received and channeled to the world through prayer. More hands or more activity do not necessarily mean more mission. The witness of Therese affirmed so strongly by the Church in the century since her death encourages us to be at the heart of the mission of the Church, whether in public ministry or totally within the monastery.

Prayer Warriors

Several Protestant churches where I live have "prayer warriors," members usually elderly and often shut-in, who have signed up to combat the work of the devil by prayer. They pray especially for physical healings and conversions. The fundamentalist packaging of this program may be problematic, but the insight is true. In Mark's gospel the ministry of Jesus is couched in terms of a war against Satan's kingdom on all fronts, and Jesus himself says some demons can be cast out only by prayer. The *Rule of Benedict* contains several descriptions of our spiritual quest in military terms, beginning with "the strong and noble weapons of obedience" (Prologue 3).

The total population of the industrialized world is becoming older because of fewer births on one side and the extension of the lifespan by medicine on the other. This is even more true of religious communities, where the rate of new members has dropped dramatically. In a society where production is everything, life beyond retirement presents a critical challenge. People who have been accustomed to self-sufficiency now find they are unable to take care of themselves, but are reluctant to become dependent on their families or anyone else. They often see themselves as useless and in the way. This can happen in the Church and even in religious life. The culture's exaltation of function over being (what I do is more important than who I am) encourages feelings of inadequacy and uselessness in the years of physical decline.

Monasticism, now especially with the emphasis by the new Doctor of the Church, has an answer for this. The power of individual lives to channel blessings to the world through hearts united to God is what monastics are about. We further believe that this does not diminish with aging, failing health, and loss of abilities—that in fact it often increases. We see it in our monastic infirmaries; but it is not limited to monasteries.

Faithful monastics who have come to the golden years grow into a state of prayer. This does not mean that they think of God all the time, but their lives are more and more focused in God. "As we progress in this way of life and in faith, we shall run on the path of God's commandments, our hearts overflowing with the inexpressible delight of love" (*RB* Prol. 49). By grace and suffering, they have been emptied of egoism, hollowed out to become channels of blessing. Though they have concern for everyone and everything that is going on, they have no great plans or demands, but by their lives are pleading to God in constant intercession. Of people like this, Thomas Merton is said to have related: "They are the tabernacles of God in the world; they are the ones who keep the universe from being destroyed; they are the little ones, they do not know themselves, but the whole earth depends on them."

For these faithful disciples, though the time of retirement seems inactive because physical exertions diminish and may be reduced to a standstill, the inner work intensifies. Even those who lose their mental faculties in the extremities of Alzheimer's disease are still interceding for the world. When practicing Catholics are unconscious from an accident, we administer the Sacrament of Anointing, presuming on their "habitual intention" to receive whatever the Church offers. A prayerful person who has entered the zone of mental incompetence likewise remains in a habitual attitude of prayer, unbroken by the failure of health. The heart that has chosen by free human actions over years to be emptied of self and filled with Christ remains fixed in that attitude and continues as a channel of God's grace for the world.

That attitude is the daily holiness offered to all of us throughout our monastic life, not just at the end. It empowers our acts and it empowers our prayer. It is the best gift monasteries can give to the world, and whether or not it is present will determine the future of monastic life in the new millennium.

Notes

This essay was originally published in *Benedictines* (Erie, PA: Saint Benedict Monastery, 1998).

1. Karl Rahner, *Theological Investigations* (New York: Seabury Press, 1990), XX, 149.
2. *The Cloud of Unknowing*. HarperCollins Spiritual Classics (San Francisco: HarperCollins, 2004), 9.
3. *Christian Prayer: The Liturgy of the Hours* (New York: Catholic Book Publishing Company, 1976).

Common Origins, 1922-1937

Gottfried Burkhard Neunheuser

Our common origins have been, without a doubt, characterized by the classic Liturgical Movement as we have seen it in the Abbey of Maria Laach in Germany, and by its coronation in the Constitution on the Sacred Liturgy of the Second Vatican Council.[1] As one of the consulters of the Commission for the realization of the Liturgical Reform,[2] desired by the Council, I witnessed the redaction of the first great document published by this "consilium" during the summer of 1964, *Inter Oecumenici*.[3] This document stated with great emphasis: "The intention of this reform is not so much to change forms and texts of the liturgy, but to obtain a pastoral activity that could make the liturgy the summit and source, and the great force of such a pastoral activity would be, *"ut mysterium paschale vivendo exprimatur,"* so that the Paschal Mystery may be expressed in life.[4]

In these words the Council clearly expressed the deepest intentions of the liturgical theology that has been the ideal for us in Maria Laach: the ideal not only during the midst of the German Liturgical Movement in 1921 when Father Damasus and I were together, but for subsequent times as well. I wish to summarize our common origins during the years 1922 until 1938 in the following way:

1918:   the beginning of the concrete liturgical apostolate in Maria Laach
1921-24: the novitiate of Damasus Winzen and Burkhard Neunheuser
1924-30: their study of philosophy and theology in San Anselmo, Rome

1928: both ordained priest in Maria Laach (August 12)
1930: both teaching philosophy in the high school of Maria Laach
1937: Father Burkhard called to Rome/San Anselmo, as professor
1938: Father Damasus called to the U.S., helping as professor
1951: foundation of Mount Saviour
1971: death of Father Damasus
1962-78: Father Burkhard: professor Pontifical Liturgical Institute, San Anselmo, Rome.[5]

Both of us had been together in the novitiate of Maria Laach. Gerd Winzen began in 1921; I came later, on September 30, 1922. However, our years before this novitiate, despite some great differences, were remarkably similar. Both of us came from universities, Winzen after many semesters in Gottingen and Munich, I after only one semester in Bonn. In addition, both of us were deeply influenced by the *Jugendbewegung,* the youth movement, and both of us had been in contact with Romano Guardini as first year students; Damasus in Munich, I in Bonn where Guardini was beginning his academic career as a professor. Guardini profoundly influenced both of us. Damasus was especially influenced by Gustau Mensching, a young Protestant philosopher, and a wonderful object of our fraternal conversations in the novitiate.[6]

But these elements disappeared, more or less, when we came as postulants, novices to the Abbey of Maria Laach. It was during these years that the monastery was actively working in the Liturgical Movement in Germany. The movement began during Easter 1918, the year in which the first volume of the anthology *Ecclesia Orans* appeared. including the article "The Spirit of the Liturgy," by Romano Guardini, with the famous introduction by Abbot Ildefons Herwegen. Under the leadership of this Abbot and the novice-master and Prior Albert Hammenstede, Father Odo Casel with all his liturgical studies, and many other monks, all worked together with the intention of actualizing the *Opus Dei,* the Liturgy of the Church, so that the mind might be in harmony with the voice (*Rule of Saint Benedict*, ch. 79).[7] Our desire was to obtain the wonderful actualization of the entire life of Maria Laach during the powerful beginning of the liturgical apostolate of the abbey, famous in Germany, Europe, and in the entire Roman Catholic Church, the work of which was finally confirmed by the Second Vatican Council in its Constitution on the Sacred Liturgy.[8]

When we arrived at Maria Laach, Father Damasus was already a mature student, a student whom we, the younger brothers, admired. I arrived after my first semester of higher studies. Both of us, indeed all of us in the novitiate, were enthusiastically open to the splendid reality of monastic/liturgical life, a life of "*Mysteriengegenwart*," the mystery-presence of Christ, the presence of the salvation work of Jesus, the Christus, the Kyrios, present in the entire celebration of the Eucharist, of the sacraments, of the Divine Office. I will try to describe this atmosphere with scientific objectivity, citing myself and others who spoke after having lived in this atmosphere.

First, allow me to repeat here what I wrote in my essay on the occasion of the one hundred-year jubilee of Maria Laach in 1993, describing the situation as it was when we arrived:

> The years 1918 to about 1926 were ones of peaceful celebration and intensive apostolic work, full of the enthusiasm of the new insight into old treasures. An expression of this mood and conviction, besides the imposing series of publications, *Ecclesia Orans*, *LQF* and *Jahrbuch fur Liturgiewissenschaft*, was a little volume of joint works, published in 1926 under the title *Mysterium Gesammelte Arbeiten Laacher Monche*. This work, small but typical in both its title and contents, can be viewed as the close of the period from 1918 to 1926, of the years of peaceful but dynamic groundwork of the Laach contribution to the liturgical movement on German soil. This work was also the beginning of the first criticism written in the essay of J.B. Umberg, the start of a scientific discussion, commonly referred to as the "controversy of

the mysteries," which was to continue for many years. It was a great time; discussion at a highly scientific level . . . conducted by significant scholars and above all by Odo Casel.[9]

In these years Father Albert Hammenstede started with the dialogue Mass, celebrated in the crypt of the Abbey Church, with the altar facing the people, famous then and famous still today.[10] Father Odo Casel wrote his great studies;[11] the entire community celebrated the liturgy according to the theological interpretation of the presence of the salvation work in it; Father Casel defended it, publishing the first synthesis of this theology in his book, *The Mystery of Christian Worship.*[12]

In later years, Abbot Ildefons Herwegen instituted for all these theological interpretations his Academy for Liturgical and Monastic Studies. But we were all passionately involved, in the sense that we supported these learned works, eagerly studying the great reply essays of Casel in *Jahrbuch fur Liturgiewissenschaft*, hoping gradually to reach an understanding and maturity of insight in the persistent effort to actualize the "presence" of the mystery of Christ in the celebration of the liturgy, in the everyday life of the monastery, and to bring this mystery to literary expression also in the works of the budding liturgical experts of the monastery."[13]

Father Damasus and I were strongly united from the very first, beginning with our theological studies in San Anselmo, Rome, and even more so through our ordination to the priesthood together on the same day, August 12, 1928, in Maria Laach. During our holidays from studies we traveled back to Laach, thus remaining in living contact with the abbot and our confreres. The abbot generously allowed us to use these travels from Rome to Maria Laach in order to visit many of the great realizations of Christian culture—Milan, Florence, Sienna, Venice, Ravenna, and even more, the great Benedictine monasteries in Italy, Switzerland, Austria, Bavaria—in order to obtain a real contact with the different forms of monastic culture during the Middle Ages and later times. Throughout these years we remained joined together, continued to grow slowly, and were in vital contact with the liturgical and theological activities of our confreres in the abbey.

From 1930 to 1938, Father Damasus and I worked together. Father Damasus worked as quasi-rector, I as a young professor in the school of philosophy, where we taught scholastic philosophy to our young confreres of Maria Laach, together with students from other abbeys of the Beuron Congregation. Our philosophical work was necessary for the theological formation of our young confreres. I have given an account of this activity in the Festschrift, *Ecclesia Lacensis*.[14] In addition, both of us were active in the theological work of the abbey: preaching retreats, speaking for different occasions, participating in the ecumenical movement of those years, and in theological publications.[15]

Our entire activity geared itself to contributing to the liturgical atmosphere of those years at Maria Laach. This activity is further described by many of the students and scholars of this period in memoirs that are still in the abbey. The most important witnesses are Salvatore Marsili, Godfrey Diekmann, Balthasar Fischer, and Johannes Pinsk.[16]

Marsili has given an excellent picture of the situation in which a young postulant was introduced in the years after 1922:

> He found himself immersed in that atmosphere of strong, and at the same time serene spirituality . . . a truly vital contact with the liturgy that the abbot Ildefons Herwegen, a man of incisive personality, was creating in the monastery. At this time, the liturgy at Maria Laach still retained the magnificent ceremonial solemnity of the era preceding the synod, and always proceeded in dignified chorus. But above all, on Sundays, the attitude of a real mystical experience took place. In general, the liturgy increased the attention to study, was the reason for apostolic work outside the monastery, and continues to remain important in the organization of the abbey and its activities.[17]

After those words of praise I would like to add still more from Godfrey Diekmann, in his descriptions of the importance given to his stays in Europe, first in San Anselmo in Rome, with professors such as Anselm Stolz, and most decisively in his encounter with Maria Laach and its world of *"Mysterien-gegenwart,"* of Spirit, where everything is full of "the presence." As I noted in a review of *The Monk's Tale*, "What he realized at that time was for Diekmann a theological synthesis, the themes were of great importance for the liturgical movement in North America."[18]

Balthasar Fischer speaks only of later years, which nevertheless typifies the past, when he says: "The atmosphere was pleasantly familiar. . . . In the first hours we indeed felt that in this man [Abbot I. Herwegen] we would get a teacher of unusual quality. Although the importance of the Laacher Academy study was not explicitly stated, most likely the most important fact was that all communal study was infused into the communal celebrated liturgy of our lectors."[19]

Finally, after these short citations, I must give the title of the book that the professors and students of the Liturgical-Monastical Academy of Maria Laach presented to Abbot Herwegen on the occasion of the silver jubilee of his abbatial election in 1938, a special volume of the journal *Liturgiches Leben*: "An honoring gift, for the celebration of the twenty-fifth anniversary of Dr. I. Herwegen, Abbot of Maria Laach, presented by teachers and students of the Monastic-Liturgical Academy of the Abbey of Maria Laach." The editor of this volume, Johannes Pinsk, a famous liturgist of these years, writes in his introduction to the book: "Since the Academy has existed now for eight years, this book is a special celebration of its first step into the public eye. It seems to me that under the special guidance of Father Damasus, published articles give a good picture of the consistent idea of the *vielseitigkent*, the many-sided characteristic, of the academic schooling of Laach."[20]

The abundant riches of this "many-sided characteristic" is easily seen in the summary given in the preface of this volume (pp. 80-81). Father Damasus was conscious of these riches when he was sent to the United States in 1938, as one of our best men, with the intention of helping Father Albert Hammen-stede search for a refuge for the Abbey in case of its suppression by Hitler.[21]

The difficulties, problems, and disappointments of these years do not belong to my essay here. What is important is that Father Damasus spoke to many excellent Catholics, both men and women, doing it with all the enthusiasm received in Maria Laach, about the "presence" of the salvation-work of Christ Jesus in the celebration of the liturgy, about the *Mysterium*. These faithful later became the oblates who convinced Father Damasus to make a foundation after the end of the war, and finally to establish the foundation of Mount Saviour.[22]

Meanwhile the two of us had already been separated in 1937, when I was called to San Anselmo in Rome to teach theology. Although we were separated, we nevertheless remained united. Through correspondence, and then by our meeting again in Rome when he came to see Pope John XXIII and also Monsignor Montini, Father Damasus's friend throughout his twenty years in Rome.

This spiritual union of ours was one of the reasons why I was invited to come to Mount Saviour after his death to put into order the correspondence of Father Damasus, especially the German letters. During the weeks of my first contact with Mount Saviour, I participated in a symposium of extraordinary quality, "Word of Silence! Spiritual Formation, East and West," an "Inter-confessional Symposium" typical of Father Damasus and the work of Mount Saviour.[23] It is not an exaggeration for me to say that this symposium was the best presentation of the intentions of the founder and of his work as the monastery tries to continue in its vocation into the next fifty years. The meeting was described as

a symposium of five days, as a congregation of representatives of the great religions . . . in a rather strict, thoroughly contemplative directed monastery, collected in silence to speak and hear reflective words about spiritual formation, contemplative prayer, and even its formal method, trying to find the common foundation that can bridge all contrasts and oppositions.[24]

This symposium was the beginning of my various travels through the United States in the following years. I tried to describe my impressions in different essays published in the review, *Beuron*, in later years.[25] Through my travels I became aware of the difference between the great abbeys as we know them in the United States and our European Congregations, and the ideal of smaller monasteries such as Mount Saviour. To be candid, I was divided in my impressions and my judgments. The great abbeys, such as Beuron and Maria Laach, had been the ideal of my monastic youth; therefore I was admiring them when I could find the same reality in the great abbeys in the States in all my travels.

I received a similar impression as well, when I saw the benefits of a smaller congregation, with its limitations, its modest scope, but also its great openness to silence, to concentration on the Spirit, to be a "Word of Silence," as the program of the symposium at Mt. Saviour in 1972 stated. Father Damasus expressed this ideal explicitly in one of his last publications in our German review, *Liturgie und Monchtum*.[26] He describes marvelously his ideal of a monastic life in its ideal purity, a so-called "contemplative" monastic life, realized in the United States. The essential features of such a monastic life could be realized also in Maria Laach after the Second Vatican Council, of course with different forms possible and necessary in our old Europe. The ideal of a monastic life in its absolute purity, can be realized now in essentially the same way, in the different concrete forms suitable to Europe and to the United States—in simplicity, in sincerity, in liveliness, open to modern reality, and more open to the Spirit of Christ, faithful to the authority *ita ut mysterium paschale vivendo exprimatur*, so that the Paschal Mystery may be expressed in life.

Notes

1. General works on Liturgical Movement include Olivier Rousseau, *Histoire du M. L.* (1959; Italian translation by Salvatore Marsili, 1961); Ferdinand Kolbe, *Die Lit. Bewegung* (1964); Bernard Botte, *Le mouvement liturgique* (Temoignage et souvenirs, 1973); Burkhard Neunheuser, *Il movimento liturgico; panorama storico e lineamenti teologici*, *Anamnesis* 1 (1974): 11-30.

2. See Piero Marini, *La nascita del "Consilium ad exsequendam Constitutionem de Sacra Liturgia"* (Gennaio-Marzo, 1964, in *Ephemerides*

Liturgicae 106 (1992): 289-318; and Marini, "*Consilium*, in Piena Attivita in un Clima Favorevole," (Ottobre 1964-Marzo 1965), in *Ephemerides Liturgicae* 109 (1995): 97-158; see my review in *Archiv fur Liturgiewissenschaft* 35/36 (1993-94), 229, and 40 (1998), 166.

3. *Inter Oecumenici* was published in *Acta Apostolicae Sedis* 56 (1964): 877-900; also in Reiner Kaczynshi, ed., *Enchiridion Documentorum Instaurationis Liturgicae* (1976), 52, nr. 203.

4. *Inter Oecumenici*, 52.

5. The information here is derived from J. Madeleva Roarke, *Father Damasus and the Founding of Mount Saviour* (Pine City, NY: Madroar Press, 1998). See also my review of this book in *Archiv fur Liturgiewissenschaft* 41 (1999).

6. See Odo Casel, "Katholische Kultprobleme," in *Jahrbuch fur Liturgiewissenschaft* 7 (1927): 105-24, critique of the booklet of G. Mensching, *Katholische Kultproble, dargestellt in ihrem Verhaltnis zur evangelischen Kultauffassung* (Gotha, 1927).

7. On Abbot Herwegen, see *Lexikon fur Theologie und Kirche*, 3, Auflage 5 (1996), 48, with his bibliography. On Prior Hammenstede, see his *Erinnerungen eines Laacher Monches. Autobiographische Aufzeichnungen*, Laacher Hefte, 2 (1996). On Father Casell and his liturgical studies, see B. Neunheuser and Odo Casel, in *Theologische Realenzyklopedie* 7 (1981): 643-48; and A. Haussling and Casel, *Lexikon fur Theologie und Kirche*, 3. *Auflage* 2 (1994): 966s; also 48; About the so-called controversy on the doctrine of Mystery, see Th. Filthaut, *Die Kontroverse uber die Mysterienlehre* (1947).

8. See *Lexikon fur Theologie und Kirche*, 3. *Auflage* 6 (1997): 992-94; my article "Maria Laach Abbey: A Double Jubilee: 1093-1993; 1892-1992," in *Ecclesia Orans* 10 (1993): 163-78, especially 166-71; and the descriptions in all the publications cited above in note 1.

9. Neunheuser, "Maria Laach Abbey: A Double Jubilee," 168f.

10. See my essay: "Die 'Kryptamesse' in Maria Laach, Ein Beitrag zur Fruhgeschichte der Gemeinschaftsmesse," in *Liturgie und Monchtum* 28 (1961): 70-82; and the scientific dissertation about the same event, Martin Conrad, *Neuansatze in der Eucharistiefeier in der Abtei Maria Laach unter Abt I. Herwegen (1913-1946)* (essentially published in *Archiv fur Liturgiewissenschaft* 41 (1999).

11. Amply presented in the dissertation of Osvaldo Santagada, *Dom Odo Casel: Contributo monografico per una Bibliografia generale delle sue opere*, in *Archiv fur Liturgiewissenschaft* 10 (1967): 7-77, with the continuation given by A. Haussling, in *Archiv fur Liturgiewissenschaft* 28 (1986): 26-42.

12. *Das Christliche Kultmysterium* (1932). The last English edition was *The Mystery of Christian Worship*, with an introduction by Aidan Kavanagh (New York: Herder and Herder, 1999).

13. Neunheuser, "Maria Laach Abbey: A Double Jubilee," 169.

14. See my essay "Die Philosophische Hochschule der Abtei Maria Laach," with special notes on the activity of Father Damasus.

15. Some examples of these activities are as follows: for Father Damasus, *Deutsche Thomas Ausgabe*, vol. 29: *Die Sakramente. Taufe und Firmung* (1935); vol. 30: *Das Geheimnis der Eucharistie* (1938); *Theology of the Kingdom of Christ*. For me, helping in the translation of the Latin texts in the *Deutsche Thomassausgabe*, vol. 29 and 30; later, *Deutsche Thomassausgabe*, vol. 31; *Sakrament der Busse* (1962); vol. 32: *Schlusselgewalt; Krankensalbung. Sakrament der Weihe* (1985). See also my bibliography in *Archiv fur Liturgiewissenschaft* 15 (1973): 123-64.

16. Salvatore Marsili, OSB, monk of the Abbey of Finalpia (Italy), abbot (1972-79), professor and 1. praeses of the Pontifical Liturgical Institute of San Anselmo/Rome. The best information on him may be found in Giustino Farnedi, *Paschale Mysterium. Studi in memoria dell' abate Prof. S.M.* (Studia Anselmiana 91, 1986). As young monk and also later as abbot he had a great friendship with Maria Laach.

Godfrey Diekmann, OSB, monk of St. John's Abbey, also visited several times during holidays and studied at the Monastic-Liturgical Academy at Maria Laach. The citations given here are taken from his biography by Kathleen Hughes, *The Monk's Tale* (Germany: Maria Laach, 1991). A short summary of this book is given in *Archiv fur Liturgiewissenschaft* 34 (1992): 223-25.

Balthasar Fischer is a priest of the diocese of Trier; he frequented the Academy in Maria Laach. He wrote an excellent description of his study on the Academy in the "Festschrift" for the jubilee of Maria Laach, edited by Emmanuel V. Severus, *Ecclesia Lacensis* (1993; cited above in note 5): 305-15. Prof. Fischer is one of the most prominent professors in the Theology Faculty of Treves (Trier).

Johannes Pinsk was a pastor in the diocese of Berlin, and also "Studenten-seeslorger" at the University of Berlin; but in both these places also an eminent liturgist. Jerzy Stefanski has written a dissertation on his liturgical work, "Il concetto di Liturgia nelle opere di Johannes Pinsk" (1972/1973). An extract with the same title was published in Rome (*Bibliotheca Ephemerides Liturgicae*, 38, 1974); also in *Eph. Lit.* 88 (1974): 81-116, and finally in a German edition "Consecratio mundi: Theologie der Liturgie bei Johannes Pinsk," *Pietas Liturgica*, Studia 7 (Pezabtei St. Ottilien: Eos-Verlag, 1990).

17. Marsili, *"Eulogia," Studia Anselmiana* 68 (1979): 5.

18. in *Archiv fur Liturgiewissenschaft* 34 (1992): 223.

19. Fischer, in *Ecclesia Lacensis*, 305, 306, 314.

20. *Liturgiches Leben* 5 (1938): 81-272; cited at 82.

21. All the details of this very complicated situation are very well described in J. Madeleva Roarke, *Father Damasus and the Founding of Mt. Saviour.* especially chapter five.

22. See Roarke, *Father Damasus and the Founding of Mt. Saviour*, 141-163 and the next chapter.

23. I have given an explicit account of this symposium in *Erbe und Auftrag* 49 (1973): 60-63. I was invited to come to arrange the German correspondence of Father Damasus, who died on 26 June 1971 in Mount Saviour.

24. In the essay cited in note 22, p. 60, I translate: "a Symposium of 5 days . . . in the house of a monastery of a rather severe, downright contemplative living formation, ready to speak a reflective work, expressed in silent concentration, but a word which is received with the intention of being foundational for spiritual formation, for contemplative prayer, trying to find the common foundation, capable to overcome all the contrary oppositions, at least a little bit."

25. "Erbe und Auftrag," *Beuron* 49 (1973): 60-63; "Ein Sommer in USA," 51 (1975): 35-42; 55 (1979): 67-70. The last visit, a longer one, from September 26-October 29, 1989, is described only in my diary.

26. In *Liturgie und Monchtum* (Laacher Hefte 43), 31-37: "Leben aus dem Geist. Gedanken bei der Erinnerung an P. Theodor Bogler." See also the excellent exposition of Father Prior Martin Boler, *The Influence of Maria Laach on Mount Saviour Monastery*, in *Ecclesia Lacencis*, 436-48, especially 436-37.

The Influence of Maria Laach on Mount Saviour Monastery

MARTIN BOLER

Moses built the tabernacle according to the pattern shown to him on the mountain. Reverend Father Damasus Winzen did the same with Mount Saviour, but his model was the monastic community of Maria Laach under the governance of Abbot Ildephonse Herwegen, with Father Albert Hammenstede as novice master. In his invitation to collaborate in this *Festschrift*, Father Emmanuel Severus suggested that I portray the goals Father Damasus had in mind when he founded Mount Saviour and something about the relations we had with Maria Laach, especially through Fathers Raphael Hombach and Burkhard Neunheuser.

The primary goal of Father Damasus never varied. It was to transplant to the United States the reality of the Catholic, monastic life he had known at Maria Laach. The concrete application would differ in certain respects; for example, a greater simplicity in all dimensions of the new monastery, its life and undertakings. If it is true that, "The apple does not fall far from the tree," it certainly applied in the case of Father Damasus and his vision of Mount Saviour, relative to Maria Laach.

Father Damasus, influenced by the monastic ideas of Abbot Ildephonse and the teaching of Father Odo Casel in the *Mysterium Christi*, wanted to establish a pneumatic monastic life in a small community without the "pomp" of pontifical liturgy. His vision of this life included the realization of the *Mysterium Christi* in the daily celebration of the Eucharist, the hours of the Office celebrated at their proper times, *Lectio Divina*, no distinction of choir monks and lay brothers, and real manual work.

In an article published in 1972, Abbot Leo Rudloff gave a succinct listing of the goals he and Father Damasus shared and discussed on their voyage to the United States in 1938.

First, America was the fertile ground for monastic renewal, for a monastery with Christian witness as its essential goal. In effect, this meant a break with parish and school work. This was not an essential departure from the basic monastic principles of our own monasteries. It would be new, of course, to existing monasteries in the United States.

Second, we intended to abandon all the romantic and medieval encrustations of our congregation and its antecedents.

Third, the celebration of the liturgy was to be central to the monastic life. The forms and structures were to reflect the times, location, and persons of the community.

Fourth, the distinction between choir-monk (priest) and lay-brother was to be abolished. Father Damasus was particularly far-sighted in this idea, considering that this centuries-old division within communities was rigidly upheld by monasteries themselves for emotional as well as economic reasons. He was also courageous, considering that canon law demanded clericalization of the monasteries. But Father Damasus cast the line firmly and neither wavered nor compromised on this explosive point.

Fifth, contingent on the above idea was the limitation of the number of priests to serve the needs of the community. This week was at the center Father Damasus's desire to return the monastic way of life to its original spirit. They were also the most controversial, since the extant monastic structure depended upon them.

Sixth, monasteries should be small in size. Bearing in mind that Maria Laach numbered 150 monks in those days, and Gerleve 90, our idea of small was around 40 or 50. Subsequently, our experience pared away that figure until it became half or even a quarter of our original thinking.

Seventh, openness was an ancient biblical concept and one practiced directly and simply by early monks. We intended to recover this Christian attitude in our monasteries by way of hospitality to guests and visitors and also by being men of our times, not of some earlier age.

There were other ideas as well as these, and even these which I mention have larger extensions, but they serve to give some notion of the original thrust of Father Damasus's thinking on the monastic life thirty years ago.

They will only be significant now in these days of *fait accompli* to those who remember when all of these insights were radical. No one could conceive of a monastery in those days that just "witnessed to the Gospels" without running parishes or schools, let alone support itself apart from the resources of those institutions. But ideas have a way of demanding existence and Father Damasus with a small group including myself was anxious to put them to the test.[1]

The ideas or goals listed above were more or less accomplished here at Mount Saviour and have become the patrimony of monastics in the years following Vatican II. In the meantime, circumstances in the United States gave rise to new goals that would be interwoven with the monastic ideals Father Damasus imbibed both at Maria Laach and during his years in Rome. They became incorporated into the fabric of the foundational goals of Mount Saviour.

Father Damasus began teaching at the major seminary of the Archdiocese of Newark, New Jersey, with Father Albert Hammenstede of Maria Laach, and Father Leo Rudloff of St. Joseph Abbey, Gerleve. Years later he would say that Father Albert loved the spirit he found in the United States, but he could not accept the lack of tradition. It is in regard to this issue that the unique contribution and insight of Father Damasus stands out most clearly.

He sensed in the seminarians, who knew little Latin and who would never be able to read a page of Augustine or Leo or Benedict in the original Latin, a spiritual hunger and a contemplative spirit that most Europeans never recognized. He saw in the laity this same receptiveness and fertile ground which filled him with surprise and joy. In a way he never expected, both groups taught him something of the deep stirrings of the Spirit in the human heart. He had learned from the Rule of Benedict that, "the Holy Spirit often speaks to the youngest" in the monastery. The one least socialized into the monastic tradition is often, in

God's plan, the one who is best able to preserve the tradition in adjusting to new circumstances. Father Damasus realized that the *doctrina* he had learned at Maria Laach was being received and responded to even more wonderfully and fruitfully by the laity than by many religious.

After three-and-a-half years of teaching at the seminary in Darlington, New Jersey, Fathers Albert, Damasus, and Leo decided to launch out on a monastic experience. They settled at Keyport, New Jersey, and called the foundation St. Paul's Priory. Later, Father Thomas Michels of Maria Laach joined this group. The foundation was problematic from the beginning, and lasted six years before it collapsed. All this time Father Damasus was extensively involved in retreat work among American religious and laity, helping in parishes, and he also became associate editor of *Orates Fratres*, now *Worship*.

In her biography of Godfrey Diekmann, Kathleen Hughes mentions the key role Father Damasus had in the Liturgical Movement in the United States:

> In 1939, Father Damasus gathered about a dozen American Benedictines, mostly friends who had met one another during their studies at, or visits to, Maria Laach. It started simply as a study group reviving the camaraderie of the "Laacher pneuma." Under the direction and enthusiasm of Father Damasus, this group became a nucleus who established Benedictine Liturgical Weeks modeled on the "Semaines Liturgiques" of Mont César. Father Damasus and his friends spelled out the purpose of the first Liturgical Week which was held in Chicago in 1940. It was to provide a common forum at which various liturgical leaders throughout the country could discuss their various problems, coordinate their efforts, and refine their methods. Second, it was to focus the interest of liturgical leaders, priests, religious generally, and as many of the local clergy and laity as possible upon the fundamental liturgical theme: "The Living Parish: Active and Intelligent Participation of the Laity in the Liturgy as Members of a Parish."

The discussions at this final Liturgical Week could not touch directly upon all liturgical problems of current interest. However, they felt if it were successful, steps could easily be taken to make it an annual affair, at which other important problems could be discussed. It was more than successful. It was a watershed event and enabled people from all over the country to come together for the first time, to pray in common, to probe issues of mutual concern as they learned from the demonstration of various rites. They met firsthand those whose articles and columns they had read, and they began to form deep and lasting friendships.[2]

This matter of friendships is most important. His friendships included people in all classes of society with a variety of educational backgrounds. He listened to them and they had a real influence on the development of his thought. His extensive involvement in the Liturgical Movement, retreat work, lecturing, and parish assistance brought him into contact with the laity on both a wider scale and more intimate basis than he experienced in Europe. Writing in a Mount Saviour newsletter, he pointed out that the Old Testament Temple was a series of exclusions. In one area, only the High Priest could enter; another was reserved for Levites and Temple personnel; another area was only for Jewish men; another court was for Jewish women; another was for the Gentiles. In the New Testament, when the faithful began to break bread in their homes, an era of inclusions was initiated. Father Damasus believed that we have not yet begun to grasp the ramifications of this significant action.

In the renovation of the chapel at Mount Saviour, the steps up to the altar were eliminated so that priests and people worship on the same level. The New Israel of the Messianic Age will live according to the "law of the house" proclaimed by Ezekiel in his description of the ideal temple and the ideal community: "This is the law of the house: up on top of the mountain the whole country! Round about in every direction is the Holy of Holies!" (Ezekiel 43:12). In the Messianic Age, the Holy of Holies ceases to be a very small place set apart to be absolutely holy. It becomes the center of sanctity in every direction. Father Damasus did not intend that monks and laity should so mix their respective vocations as to dilute either, but that there would be an inbuilt reciprocity to strengthen each. Father Damasus loved to quote the response of Cardinal Montini (soon to become Pope Paul VI) when Father Damasus told him about founding Mount Saviour: "Open the doors, Dammaso, open the doors!"

The best summation of the first part of this paper on the goals of Father Damasus in founding Mount Saviour and the goals or vision he had near the end of his life are in this excerpt of a conference he gave to the Mount Saviour community:

> I have always considered this aspect of the teaching of Abbot Ildefonse as basic for Mount Saviour: the mind in harmony with the voice (*mens concordet voci*), not to rattle down the office as fast as possible but to pray it with understanding, not as an expression of individual moods but as a growing into the ever deeper understanding of the God-given voice, or Word. The "words of eternal life," as the creative pronouncement or proclamation of God's saving design, which Scripture calls the *mysterium*: Christ, his death and resurrection, his *agape*.
>
> The daily being "exposed" to the riches of Christ, to his power of the Resurrection in *lectio* and in the celebration of the sacraments I considered, following the teachings of Maria Laach, as the principal transforming power and for the individual monk. In the course of the years, however, it became more and more clear to me that more is needed for the monk to achieve his goal, namely systematic practice of the spiritual art, but in a realistic and human way. That means that all "perfectionism" should be avoided. We are not angels. As men, every one of us carries the burden of his inborn character. This we should come to accept, which is the central act of humility. Our character will never essentially change. It will always stamp our first reactions. The work of the Holy Spirit starts only where the immediate reactions

end. These are the material with which the Spirit works in and through our "second reactions." These again are not based on our natural virtues (or will-power), but on Christ who lives in us through faith. Faith in Christ means to believe that He has loved us first, that we are sheltered in His love, because He loves us to the end, and that in His infinite love He knows us better than our heart. He knows everything. We are known by Him, not with the knowledge of the detective, but with His loving knowledge, covering a multitude of sins. In this faith in Christ's loving knowledge we become our true selves, although it will never be manifest what we really are as long as we live in this body, or in this world. But we are able in the power of Christ's love for us to believe, to trust in our salvation, "in the shadow of His wings." This faith should prevent us from getting stuck in the immediate reactions in us against the immediate reactions of our brothers. It is only natural that, for example, arrogance on the part of a brother would draw the immediate reaction of anger on our part, especially when there is much arrogance in ourselves. But again, this reaction is only natural, immediate, automatic, and it should be considered as such by myself and by all, so that then the spell, the infection of our natural reaction could be broken either by ourselves or by our brother. We may then say that these two things should be working at Mount Saviour to make it a "holy community," exposing all monks to the saving power of Christ as it is working in word and sacrament, and systematic effort on the part of every brother, alone as well as in community, to react and to live, beyond the sphere of the immediate reactions, which should be taken for granted, out of that peace and strength and truth, which our faith in Christ's first love of us opens up for all.[3]

Permission for the foundation of Mount Saviour was granted by the Congregation for Religious in Rome on October 11, 1950. The reality of founding a new monastery proved far more difficult than Father Damasus had been able to foresee. In July of 1952, he had a serious nervous breakdown that required hospitalization and then a year's absence from the monastery. He returned in August of 1953. This illness proved to be a turning point in his life, and it was to some lay friends that he gives credit for his recovery. Survival of the monastery became the primary goal, and we hear no more of the lesser goals that had previously occupied his mind.

In the years preceding his breakdown, considerable inner tension developed between his spiritual inheritance from Maria Laach and the new ideas that had taken root and found nourishment in the United States. He tried to do justice to the ideals of Maria Laach, while simultaneously objecting to an overemphasis on the sacramental life, which he felt brought the objective and esthetic aspects of spirituality too much to the fore. He believed that one could develop a false sense of security that placed too strong an accent on the new nature gained from baptism and ordination. This can go so far that one takes grace for granted. He told some friends that the experience of the breakdown led him to new insights about the necessity of an ever-repeated new beginning, of a determined turning towards Christ. It had to be done systematically by taking all the small steps required. St. Benedict's expression of a "School of the Lord's Service" prompted Father Damasus to call the method of returning to the peace that Christ has with the Father in the Spirit, and to which we have access, "The School of the Heart."

Professor Balduin Schwarz gives a beautiful account of the School of the Heart in the issue of *Monastic Studies* referred to above. I would like to quote from his article not only for the light it throws on the nature of this "method," but as a tribute to the debt Father Damasus owed to the laity and to its importance as a "legacy" for us as monks and for the laity:

> Developed by lay people not living in a community who, however, feel called to make the spirit of St. Benedict the inner form of their lives, The School does not concern itself with the monastic obedience in the specific sense of obedience to a superior in regulating one's daily dispositions. Nor does it deal with the Rule of St.

Benedict as containing a set of specific "rules and regulations" ordering the community life, but only as this great book shows a "spirit." In the Rule that spirit is applied to particular situations, but also expressed in general observations and "admonitions"—particularly in the Prologue. The spirit of the holy Rule—such is the basic assumption—is equally valid in a monastery and in the world, that is, under conditions of life where few or none of the specific regulations could or should be followed to the letter. St. Benedict wants his monks to become true Christians, and what he had to say about that tremendous concern "how to become a Christian" is of great import for us who live in the world.

Furthermore, neither the holy Rule nor the School—which tries to make transparent for us something of the spirit of the Rule—are concerned with the basic decision which makes a Christian, the decision to follow Christ. The totality implied in the call to follow Christ, and the plenitude of life which opens up to one who wants in earnest to heed that call, are not spelled out, they are only hinted at in the Rule. They are not the topic of the School. It is rather a question of how to go about following the call of Christ as realistically as possible. The great stress laid by St. Benedict on the removal of obstacles for the full unfolding of the divine life in our souls is taken up in the School.

St. Benedict sees the life of a true Christian—and that is what he wants his monk to become—as *servitium*, a service. This is basic for the spirit of the Rule. St. Benedict considers in the very first paragraph the one "to whom my words are now addressed, whosoever you may be," as willing "to fight for the true king, Christ," to serve him by "taking up the strong and glorious weapons of obedience." This is to be understood very specifically and needs some close scrutiny, for what is meant here was probably more obvious to those who lived in the sixth century; the figure of speech is more remote from our way of thinking, and may even have wrong connotations.

In speaking of "service" there is a presupposition underlying which is nowhere explicitly stated in the holy Rule, yet is everywhere present: to live as a Christian means to have the strong belief that Christ is the master of my own life, so that I desire to live that life in its totality and in every aspect not only according to his commandments (that is understood) but in my every move and plan, in what I desire and what I decide—and all this as concretely as possible. Christ has his plans for me. They are plans of life and it is my desire to come to know them, without illusions, as closely as I can, and to follow them. To serve Christ means certainly no blind, servile submission—it is a kingly service, according to the word of the liturgy: *Servire Deo regnare est*. It is the liberation of our true self from the servitude of our fallen nature. In this sense "to serve God means to reign." This "freedom of the children of God" is obtained through obedience—perhaps the keyword of the holy Rule—obedience to the divine will. Monastic obedience to a superior is but a means for the realization of that basic obedience to God.

In the early fifties I was privileged to discuss these matters intensively with Reverend Father Damasus, in almost daily conversations. He was greatly interested in the experiences and ideas of those who put into practice this attempt to "translate" the holy Rule into counsels and reflections applying to our time. He shared the experience and took part in its development.

Reverend Father Damasus considered the School, though conceived for lay people, equally applicable to the monastic life as lived by a monk, though it has, of course, to be amended by other factors specific to the life in a monastery.[4]

Having written about Father Damasus's unique contribution to the *doctrina abbatis* of Abbot Ildephonse, which he transmitted to the community of Mount Saviour, I want to say something about how the spirit of Maria Laach influenced our community life at Mount Saviour. It happened in much the same way as the life of the community that formed around the historical Jesus. Jesus sent out disciples two by two. One person is not a community but two can be. For us at Mount Saviour, it was Father Damasus and Father Raphael Hombach at one time and Father Damasus and Father Burkhard Neunhauser at another.

Father Raphael first came to Mount Saviour on May 20, 1960, and he was with us until September 25. It is impossible to convey to those who never have been in the same situation what it means for young and inexperienced monks to have the companionship of an older experienced monastic. It is not only true of Father Albert Hammenstede that the lack of tradition is frightening or at least profoundly unsettling, it was also true for us. We had no "gray heads" and the need for experience and wisdom has always plagued us. Father Raphael's presence gave us a much needed solidity and sense of rootedness in monastic tradition at a time when it was most needed and appreciated. During his first visit, we experienced the first death of a member of our community, Br. Christopher Claas. He died suddenly while reading to the community at the noon meal.

The shock to all of us, and to Father Damasus in particular, was greatly alleviated by the presence of Father Raphael, a beloved confrere who was like a solid rock to Father Damasus, and Father Raphael handled all the liturgical details of the first funeral. By taking this burden from us, we were enabled to participate in the death and resurrection of the Lord into which our brother was now fully entering. My own ordination to the priesthood took place less than a week after Brother Christopher's death, and I am eternally grateful for Father Raphael's help and humor.

Father Raphael returned again a year later on September 6, 1961, and, except for a brief trip to Rome, was with us until September of 1962. It was during this visit that he made what we affectionately refer to as the Rafaelian Reform of our Liturgy. He also rearranged the psalms, which was a most significant step in the reform of the monastic breviary. It deserves some comment here.

St. Benedict had recommended changing the order of the psalms, as long as the full complement of 150 psalms were said each week.

According to his arrangement 246 psalms were recited each week because of the number of repetitions. Over the centuries monks departed from many of the prescriptions of the Rule, but the one area in which our holy father Benedict gave permission to change, no one touched. As a result, the order and number of psalms in the Benedictine Office had so rusted in place that no one could even imagine changing them. One of the arguments put forth at a Congress of Abbots and Priors in Rome was that the arrangement of the Divine Office was the only thing Benedictine monks had in common. To change the arrangement of the psalter would shatter the Benedictine Confederation irreparably.

It is impossible to recreate the climate of the time, and so it is impossible to fully appreciate Father Raphael's pioneering work in the necessary reform of the breviary. No matter how cogent the reasons for change, including St. Benedict's explicit instructions to do so, the order of the psalmody had become sacrosanct. The change had to come first, and only then would the reasons seem fitting. A well established monastery could not have made any change because of internal and external resistance. Someone lacking the erudition of Father Raphael would have ruined the undertaking and his being able to do the work at a small, insignificant, independent monastery made all the difference. A number of other factors, such as an adequate library, the financial help and encouragement of Abbot Bonaventure Knaebel and the monks at St. Meinrad Archabbey, as well as several other contributors were vitally important. Finally, the approval of Church authorities such as Cardinal Laarona enabled the experiment to be carried on in spirit and in truth, openly and officially.

Father Raphael's work was finished and published in 1962, before the opening of Vatican II and long before the document on the Sacred Liturgy released in December 1963. Father Raphael used the arrangement of psalms in the Roman Office of the fifth and sixth centuries and compared it with St. Benedict's revision of the psalmody. Father Raphael's arrangement was based on St. Benedict's direction to "by all means" carefully maintain 150 psalms every week.

A second printing included a bolder step of a schema without the office of Prime. A small eight-page booklet, entitled "Notes on the Proposed Redistribution of the Psalter," accompanied the *Psalterium Monasticum ad Experimentum Novo Dispositum*, which was widely and freely distributed to Benedictine and other religious institutes throughout the world. Copies of this booklet are available in the archives of the various monasteries that received copies of Father Raphael's work. In his last paragraph, Father Raphael anticipates the mind of the Council Fathers and the Holy Spirit at Vatican II by stating that his intention was "to respond to present day needs . . . and be consistent with the spirit of the Rule of our Holy Father, St. Benedict." Paragraph two of *Perfectae Caritatis* reads:

> The appropriate renewal of religious life involves two simultaneous processes: (1) a continuous return to the sources of all Christian life and to the original inspiration behind a given community and (2) an adjustment to the changed conditions of the time.

I do not want to imply that Vatican II or the reform of the monastic office could not have taken place without the work of Father Raphael at Mount Saviour Monastery. The Holy Spirit could have found myriads of other ways to bring about reform of the monastic office and Vatican II. What I do want to say is that, in part, the work of many scholars at Maria Laach, Abbot Ildephonse among them, in the context of community life there produced the climate in which monks like Father Raphael could come to a knowledge of spirituality and liturgy that enabled them to recognize the need for reform of the office and equipped them to respond in line with the doctrine of St. Benedict. But the existence of Mount Saviour, whose prior was a monk of Maria Laach and whose community gave a context in which Father Raphael was free to do the research and accomplish the project, provided the means that the Holy Spirit did use. Finally, the reputation and integrity of both monasteries enabled others to contribute financially and confidently to a project that was worthy of their necessary support and ultimately received approval from the highest authority in the Church. It was a wonderful work of God for which we give everlasting thanks with humble pride.

There are many other things I could write about Father Raphael and how as a monk of Maria Laach he influenced our lives. His impish humor, the hikes in the Catskill mountains, his humanity shown in his appreciation of culture, my own trips with him to New York City and to the blessing of Abbot Alban Boultwood in Washington, D.C. are but a few memories that come to mind. For the purpose of this article on this occasion, our focus has been on the important work he did in the reform of the Divine Office and to give some indication of how together with Father Damasus he handed on to us something of the brotherhood and spirit of Maria Laach.

I also want to say a few words about another monk of Maria Laach to whom we owe much, Father Burkhard Neunheuser. Father Burkhard's first visit was from August 27 until September 8, 1963. It was most memorable for a visit to Woodstock Maryland, home of the most vibrant Jesuit theologate in the East. Father John Courtney Murray and Father Avery Dulles were among its faculty. Some of the young monks were wondering what a Jesuit was and thought a good first step was to find out what a Jesuit was not. In order to do so, they invited a Benedictine, a Carmelite, and a Trappist. They invited enough Jesuit provincials to prevent a full scale decampment and put us all together. Father Damasus had been invited as the Benedictine, but he convinced them that Father Burkhard would be a better representative. Gatherings of Roman Catholic religious were very rare in those days, and this was a wonderful experience. Some lifelong friendships were established and because of Father Burkhard's performance, we were very proud to be Benedictines.

His second visit was from July 28 until September 27, 1972. In late August through early September of that year, we had a symposium entitled "Word Out of Silence." It brought together religious leaders of the various world religions. We had Sufis, Swamis, Buddhists, and Jewish Hassidic representatives as well as Orthodox Jews, Orthodox Archimandrites, representatives of various Protestant churches, and some non-descript "Eastern" groups, whose members were formerly Catholic or at least Christian. They all lived at Mount Saviour. We did not allow anyone to bring an entourage of disciples and the other participants were carefully selected to include abbots, academics in the field of spirituality, monks with similar qualifications, and graduate students we thought would profit from the symposium and be able to contribute to it.

It was the first gathering of this kind. We avoided publicity, since we wanted the participants to be able to talk to one another without the need to be on guard because of the presence of their devotees or the presence of the media. It was a tremendous success, but that is another story. It is the contribution of Father Burkhard in the success of the meeting that I wish to convey.

This symposium was like the first space voyage; it was without precedent, and without known boundaries. Since I bore the ultimate responsibility for whatever happened, you can imagine the support afforded by a monk of Maria Laach, well grounded in the faith, an expert in liturgy, a *peritus* at Vatican II, and so experienced in dealing with enormous egos. It was a very volatile situation and all the tact, prudence, wisdom, and courage available was needed. Without Father Burkhard the event would have exploded like the Challenger spacecraft. Yet an event like this, when it takes place in a monastery where the Paschal Mystery and the Agape of God in Christ are the focus of life, has an entirely different impact on the lives of the participants and ultimately the world at large than when it happens in any other context.

Since Father Damasus had died in June, 1971, our need for direction and confidence in what we were doing was all the greater. The symposium was a rite of passage for all who attended. Father Burkhard's subtle and gentle influence is what kept us properly focused.

During a three week visit in September of 1974, Father Burkhard gave us a series of lectures on the work of Father Odo Casel and on the liturgy. The next year in July, Father Burkhard gave us eight conferences on the preface to the *Thesaurus Liturgiae Horarum Monasticae*. Father Raphael and Father Burkhard always took part in our community recreations and outings, much to our delight and edification. Once we took several canoes down the Chemung River, which flows past our property. Father Burkhard was in the care of the two most vocal experts in this Indian art. They tipped over three times, which can be a very disastrous accident in a fast flowing river which hides fallen trees that can snare an ankle or an arm. Nothing seemed to dampen Father Burkhard's enthusiasm.

On his fifth visit, in September, 1982, Father Burkhard gave us very valuable conferences on the history of Maria Laach and its role in the liturgical revival. He and I attended the ordination of Bishops Emerson Moore and Patrick O'Keefe in St. Patrick's Cathedral in New York City. It was an unbounded joy for him to witness, in another culture, the results of the work of the liturgical commissions on which he had served becoming incarnate in the celebration of these ordinations. For me and for all of us with whom he shared the experience, it was a great lesson in the value of patient study, long and difficult discussions, temporary discouragement, and all the difficulties that make up any important enterprise. Father Burkhard was able to make one final visit two years later on his return from presenting a series of conferences in South America.

It is our understanding that Abbot Ildephonse desired a holy community and not an association of individual stars. Father Damasus and a confrere, at one time Father Raphael and at another Father Burkhard, formed a holy community like the disciples sent out by our Lord. In large measure that is how we learned our monastic fundamentals, the *schola servitii Domini*, St. Benedict intended.

At the end of his life, Father Damasus wrote: "When I look back on the seventy years of my own life, I see quite clearly that I owe my present inner happiness, my peace, my confidence, and my joy essentially to one single fact: I am certain that I am infinitely loved by God."

That was not an insight of recent origin. The seed, the root, the trunk, the branches, and a good deal of the fruit had already grown at Maria Laach.

Notes

1. Abbot Leo Rudloff, "In Memory of Father Damasus," *Monastic Studies* 8 (spring 1972): 7-8.

2. Kathleen Hughes, *The Monk's Tale: A Biography of Godfrey Diekmann, O.S.B.* (Collegeville, MN: The Liturgical Press, 1991), 123ff.

3. Father Damasus Winzen, from a conference at the monastic community of Mount Saviour, Pine City, NY, 1951.

4. Balduin Schwarz, "The School: On Benedictine Spirituality in Our Time," *Monastic Studies* 8 (spring 1972): 26ff.

The Art of Christian and Monastic Life

TIMOTHY KELLY

In St. Matthew's Gospel, when Jesus was talking about the coming of the Son of Man and the time of his coming, he talked about the signs that will indicate that the time is near. Then he said the following: "Take the fig tree as a parable: as soon as its twigs grow supple and its leaves come out, you know that summer is near. So with you when you see these things: know that he is near, right at the gates" (Matthew 24:32-33).

My paper focuses on the sign value of human, Christian, and monastic life. I was born into a Christian and Catholic family. As a Benedictine monk who entered monastic community forty-seven years ago, I have spent a lot of that time trying to make sense of it as an expression of the meaning of Christian life. I have pondered it as a Christian, monk, student, priest, teacher, missionary, pastor, prison chaplain, convent chaplain, director of novices, and an abbot, among other things. If Jesus could tell people to look for the signs of the coming of the Son of Man, then I can say I have spent my life looking for those signs that give meaning to my life as a Christian and as monk.

I have to admit that my best insights have come as the result of others who have had an impact on my life. It always amazes me how God speaks profoundly in the simplest of signs. It is this experience that teaches us to pay attention to the more intentional signs God has given us. In fact, God has gone to great lengths to get us to know God. The signs are all around us.

Let's move directly to the heart of God's sign-giving: humanity made in the image and likeness of God in us has nothing to do with physical appearance, gender, color, size, or language. It also does not mean that we are just like God. That would be impossible. According to St. Thomas Aquinas, God is of an entirely different order of being. God is without limit, and in our order of being, to be means to have boundaries. So we are made in the image and likeness of God in a different way, and when we live in accord with the truth of our being, we are then living revelations of who God is.

Dietrich Bonhoeffer, the German Lutheran pastor and theologian who had the integrity to be martyred rather than submit to the abominations of Nazi theory and practice, gave a series of lectures in the early 1930s that were subsequently published in a small book called *Creation and Fall*. In a nutshell, he said that God created not out of necessity but freely, and that nothing has the power to so much as tempt God to betray creation. Bonhoeffer put it in terms of freedom: God is free for creation, and free from what would make God stop being for creation. Bonhoeffer equated God's freedom with God's love. The image and likeness of God in humanity is that love, that freedom for the other, the freedom from whatever might destroy love for one another. In short, for Bonhoeffer the image and likeness of God that becomes the clearest sign and revelation of the reality of God is humanity in unity. Adam and Eve in the Genesis stories represent the totality of humanity in unity with all their diversity, not just the individualistic notion that each person is the image and likeness of God apart from activating that gift.

Now we all know about the fall. So let's go directly to the solution. One of the best summaries of God's plan for us in Christ is found in the Letter to the Colossians:

He is the image of the unseen God,
the first-born of all creation,
for in him were created all things
in heaven and on earth:
everything visible and everything invisible,
thrones, ruling forces, sovereignties, powers —
all things were created through him and for him.

He exists before all things
and in him all things hold together,

and he is the Head of the Body,
that is, the Church.

He is the Beginning,
the first-born from the dead,
so that he should be supreme in every way;
because God wanted all fullness to be found in him
and through him to reconcile all things to him,
everything in heaven and everything on earth,
by making peace through his death on the cross.
(Colossians 1:15-20)

What was torn apart by sin, what lessened the effectiveness of the sign of humanity as the image and likeness of God, is now reconciled in Christ, who is head of the reconciled body of humanity. In him who is "the image of the unseen God" we in our reconciled unity might become that people who reveal God with us by our love for one another as members of the Body of Christ, the church. In other words, we are God's "are," God's living art.

No art perfectly expresses the mind and the heart of the creator of that art, and that is why artists keep on producing more art. The Christian community, this Body of Christ, is constantly demonstrating that it is not just like God. So we make God known in halting ways, but ways that nevertheless give hope to all of humanity. We love one another as Christ has loved us, and ask forgiveness and forgive when we have failed. We get married in Christ so that the unity in diversity in marriage will announce and be the sign of Christ's love for the Church. We gather into intentional communities of faith, some of which are monastic, so that by the witness of inclusive love the world might know God's inclusive love. This too is the art, the living art of God.

As Christians, whether monk, married, or single, we have a common goal built on our relationship to Christ Jesus. Everything in our life is centered on Christ. The history and mystery of our salvation is Christ. The whole of creation is through and for Christ. The love of God for us even precedes creation, and creation itself is the first manifestation and even contains the love of God for all people. Creation is the demonstration of God's love and God's will to include all people everywhere and in every age in the salvation that God wants all to share in.

When we look about the world we see the murderous disunity that on close examination we can discover in our immediate environment and even within our own selves. Some people seeing that in themselves hate themselves. Others allow this disunity to overflow in their relationships to those nearest them. Others expand this division to whole nations and then to the world.

We are invited to "know the mystery of his [God's] purpose, according to his good pleasure which he determined beforehand in Christ" (Ephesians 1:9). We are to look at God's plan established prior to creation so that we might understand the purpose of creation and in our hearts accept one another and all people because God excludes no one. We are not a select elite among the few who will be saved. That would be contrary to the message God gives to us. The separation from one another that sin produces is overcome in God's plan that God "would bring everything together under Christ, as head, everything in the heavens and everything on earth" (Ephesians 1:10).

What I am describing here is called "Paschal [Easter] spirituality." What that means is that because we are centered on Christ, because we have been baptized into his death and resurrection, we have a new life. The monastic community is meant to be a sign to the whole Church, to all of creation, of the reconciliation Christ has accomplished and makes known through what I dare to call the "sacrament of monastic life." If married life is a sacrament, the sign, the living revelation of the faithful union between Christ and the Church, then monastic life is to reveal the diversity that can come together in unity in Christ.

The Benedictine monk vows stability, that is, fidelity to the community; *conversatio*, or living the covenant of this monastic manner of life; obedience, or hearing God's call, Word, message through the scriptures, the Church, the community, the superiors, through each other. And the monk does this by living the reality of the Paschal Mystery today.

It takes a real effort to apply the theory of Paschal spirituality to all areas of life. Yet it is the only spirituality that can help us to make sense of life. It involves confronting the most basic realities of life so that we learn to see them as parts of our journey with Christ to the accomplishment of God's purpose in us. There is nothing of reality that can stand outside of the Paschal Mystery that describes God's love for us and our response to God.

There is in this the acceptance of ourselves, as difficult as that can sometimes be: acceptance of ourselves from the weakness of childhood, through the strength of maturity, to the weakness of life's end when we give up all power. We also acknowledge the reality of our necessary interrelatedness and the fact that we do live in this world with others, and that the goal of all is to be fostered and protected by all so that all, through Christ's reconciliation, might come together to the fulfillment of God's plan of salvation.

The only way this can be accomplished is through mutual love, which reveals God's covenant with all of humanity, excluding none. By this covenant God reveals faithfulness, and by living in that covenant we are telling all people: I am here for you. I will not abandon you. I will die rather than betray you. You can count on me. There we have the behavioral evidence that we are living the Paschal Mystery by the total gift of ourselves to God. We cannot ever separate our dedication to God from our relationship to the very real humanity our lives touch every day.

The way we treat one another infallibly reveals our relationship to God. We cannot compartmentalize our spiritual life as though it has no relationship to the way we live with others for the good of all in this world. If it takes real effort to apply Paschal spirituality to all areas of life, it is because we find reconciliation and outreach so trying. Living the covenant that Paschal spirituality implies involves every moment of life.

The monastic community is a presence in this world of people who strive to have some understanding of this Paschal spirituality in order to live it in such a manner that in a deceitful and underhand world we might shine out "like bright stars in the world, proffering to it the Word of life" (Philippians 2:15-16). Long hours in prayer and daily *lectio* may well be essential for the monk to live the Paschal Mystery, but the evidence that we are doing so will always be our faithfulness to the covenant we have freely entered into, by which we say: I am here for you. It is the actual living together, the encounter with fellow human beings, the mutual support, the encouragement, the forgiveness for wrongs done, the hospitality within and outside the community, the "supporting with the greatest patience one another's weaknesses of body or behavior" (*RB* 72:5) that become for the monk the font of revelational experience of the living God in our midst. Monastic life is first a living experience of God in community.

The Role of *Lectio Divina*

Lectio divina, or holy reading, is both a practice and a way of life. As a practice it typified monastic life. Scripture is normative for the monk as it is for all Christians, and St. Benedict directs us in these words:

> For anyone hastening on to the perfection of monastic life, there are the teachings of the holy Fathers, the observance of which will lead him to the very heights of perfection. What page, what passage of the inspired books of the Old and New Testaments is not the truest of guides for human life? What book of the holy catholic Fathers does not resoundingly summon us along the true way to reach the Creator? Then, besides the Conferences of the Fathers, their Institutes and their Lives, there is also the rule of our holy father Basil. For observant and obedient monks, all these are nothing less than tools for the cultivation of virtues. (*RB* 73:2-6)

The monk is to be immersed in the Word of God, for it is the Word of God who gives us life.

We can look at St. Benedict's own experience as given to us in the Dialogues of St. Gregory the Great. The story of Benedict begins with his disillusionment with the environment he found himself in while pursuing studies in Rome. It seems clear that he came from a decent family background, had a religious sense about him, and had no desire to compromise his dedication to God by living in the manner of other students:

When he found many of the students there abandoning themselves to vice, he decided to withdraw from the world he had been preparing to enter; for he was afraid that if he acquired any of its learning he would be drawn down with them to his eternal ruin. In his desire to please God alone, he turned his back on further studies, gave up home and inheritance and resolved to embrace the religious life. He took this step, fully aware of his ignorance; yet he was truly wise, uneducated though he may have been.[1]

When eventually Benedict would go to Monte Cassino and write his *Rule*, he would do so with an eye to establishing an environment that would not be an escape from the world but an alternative and mutually supportive way of living in the world while seeking God. In chapter one of the *Rule*, when he speaks of the different kinds of monks, he tells us that he wishes "to draw up a plan for the strong kind, the cenobites" (*RB* 1:13). These are monks "who belong to a monastery, where they serve under a rule and an abbot" (*RB* 1:2). The monastery is the environment in which the tools for good works can be employed, for "the workshop where we are to toil faithfully at all these tasks is the enclosure of the monastery and stability in the community" (*RB* 4:78).

We can hardly look at the Rule and not come away convinced that the vast majority of what Benedict has to say is dealing with the building of an environment that supports seeking God and enables the monks to encourage one another in this pursuit of holiness. The many chapters devoted to outlining the *opus dei* and the practice of *lectio divina* are a major focus for this environment. His structuring of community meetings for the sake of communal discernment, of meal times with reading, of work that supports the community, of silence that allows for listening, of deans and priors for the sake of good discipline, of respect for the goods of the monastery, of excommunication for faults that do harm to the environment of seeking God—all of these point to an emphasis on creating the atmosphere in which blocks to seeking God are minimized and encouragement for growth in holiness is maximized.

Benedict would set a schedule of daily prayer when the monks coming together would praise God. He did so, not because only these were the prayer times for the monks, but rather to sanctify all times, because we are to pray always. He established an oratory where this work of God and Eucharist would be celebrated, a place where nothing else was to be done. He did this to recognize a sacred space that announces to the monks that all space is sacred, and he even calls the monastery the house of God. He indicates the sacredness of all objects as well by declaring that the tools of the monastery are to be treated as the sacred vessels of the altar. What a wonderfully holistic view Benedict had of the monastery, this school of the Lord's service.

When we get right down to it, Benedict had a pretty good notion of what goes into the makeup of a human being. Maybe it has taken us longer to learn a simple rule: garbage in, garbage out. If we are what we eat, we should have no trouble understanding that we become what we do, what we read, what we listen to and watch. We know that to become anything good we have to study, to absorb, to want to learn, to discipline ourselves. *Lectio* as a practice is necessary if we would live a life of *lectio*, if we would be formed by the Word of God, if we would become assimilated to the Christ who become one with us that we might become one with God.

So we read and are read to; we listen to the Word of God with the ears of our heart so that we might return to him from whom we had drifted by the sloth of disobedience. Obedience means hearing, and disobedience means not hearing, not listening to the voice of God calling us and saying,

"Is there anyone here who yearns for life and desires to see good days?" If you hear this and your answer is "I do," God then directs these words to you: "If you desire true and eternal life, keep your tongue free from vicious talk and your lips from all deceit; turn away from evil and do good; let peace be your guest and aim. Once you have done this, my eyes will be upon you and my ears will listen for your prayers; and even before you ask me, I will say to you: 'Here I am' " (*RB*, Prologue 15-18).

Now, the problem with listening is that we become responsible for what we hear. And when we immerse ourselves in the scriptures, two things will happen to us. First, we will become aware of the message of the scriptures. By this I do not mean that we become expert exegetes who can grapple with the historical, cultural, and philological problems the experts tackle. Rather, we become experientially aware of God speaking, inviting us to recognize the Word through whom all came to be, and that nothing that is came to be in any other way than through God's Word. We begin to see more and more the unity of creation, and especially our unity in humanity that should become ever more clearly the image of God on earth.

This, in turn, confronts us in our relationship not only to God but to the people around us and around the world. If we experience ourselves as coming forth from the love of God, we have to see our neighbor in the same light: "How can you love the God you do not see if you do not love the neighbor whom you do see?" The love of God and the love of neighbor grow side by side. As the vision of our neighbor-as-Christ grows so does our vision of God grow. And this is when the second problem presents itself.

It is one thing to be Word-centered with a capital W, another to be word-centered with a small w. (Friends, this has absolutely nothing to do with politics and our current president!) We tend to overuse words as though they could "contain" reality in and of themselves. We encapsulate God in words as though we could control God, tame God, carry God around in our back pocket or handbag. And finally, painfully, we discover that God eludes us and refuses to be imprisoned in our concepts. We can't even do this to one another, no matter how much we think our psychologizing and Myers-Briggs tests and Enneagrams and Minnesota Multiple Personality Inventories tell us about others. We still remain a mystery, and all the more does God.

Saint John of the Cross said, in *The Ascent of Mount Carmel*: "The soul will have to empty itself of these images and leave this sense in darkness if it is to reach divine union. For these images, just as the corporeal objects of the exterior senses, cannot be an adequate, proximate means to God" (12.4). Words and images are insufficient to carry the reality of God; they can only point in a direction and open us to what we cannot imagine. "What no eye has seen and no ear heard, what the mind of man cannot visualize; all that God has prepared for those who love him" (1 Corinthians 2:9).

In speaking of Byzantine theology, John Meyendorff says:

> Theology . . . may and should be based on Scripture, on the doctrinal decisions of the Church's magisterium, or on the witness of the saints. But to be a true theology, it must be able to reach beyond the letter of Scripture, beyond the formulae used in definitions, beyond the language employed by the saints to communicate their experience. For only then will it be able to discern the unity of Revelation, a unity which is not simply an intellectual coherence and consistency, but a living reality experienced in the continuity of the one Church throughout the ages: the Holy Spirit is the only guarantor and guardian of this continuity; no external criterion which would be required for man's created perception or intellection would be sufficient.[2]

Interestingly enough, although Taoism asserts that the underlying reality of all is "so vast that it cannot be described in words," the Chicago Institute of Art hosted an exhibition entitled "Taoism and the Arts of China." And though St. John of the Cross could say that the "soul will have to empty itself of these images and leave this sense in darkness if it is to reach divine union," we will nevertheless use an abundance of words to explain this and will even sketch an unusually beautiful and perceptive crucifixion of Jesus that he presented to someone else.

Similar to marriage, so too monastic life is a gift to the whole Church, a witness that is visible of certain Christian values that speak to the world something of who God is and what it means to live as faithful witnesses of God revealing God in ways visible to the human experience. Edward Schillebeecks entitled one of his books *Christ, the Sacrament of the Encounter with God*.[3] We might say that married life is a sacrament of encounter with Christ, not only for one another but for the whole Church who sees the meaning of faithful love as revealed in Christ. We can also say that monastic life is another sacrament, at least by analogy, of the encounter with Christ that represents the broader reconciliation of humanity in Christ.

Liturgy

Some may find it offensive to stretch the meaning of sacrament beyond the defined seven sacraments of the Roman Catholic and Orthodox Church. However, I would submit that if we cannot do that stretch we impoverish the meaning of sacrament, and in the process lose the meaning of liturgy. Let me explain.

At the age of four, a little boy goes to a vacant lot next door, picks a bouquet of odd weeds, and brings them home to his mother as a sign of his love for her. She takes the weeds, places them in a vase with water, and sets them on the dining room table. As other members of the family return home from school or work, she warns them at the door: "You call those weeds and I'll annihilate you." A four year old boy gave his mother a sacrament, a sign of his love, and she accepted it. Here has been played out a family liturgy.

The Baltimore Catechism called a sacrament an "outward sign." Now a sign that is not outward is no sign at all. By nature we are sign givers, we are sacramental, and we understand the meaning and effectiveness of signs. In his Rule, St. Benedict unerstood the meaning of such signs and clearly went beyond words only. At liturgy in common he recognized the value of bowing and prostrations; when receiving guests, of washing their feet, praying with them, and only then giving them the sign of peace. He understood the reverence needed between the monks: seniors are to love their juniors and juniors are to reverence their seniors. All of these are accompanied by signs and liturgies that are visible and recognizable. The whole monastic life, then, is a liturgy, a sign or even a sacrament that is visible and recognizable.

Within the monastic living situation there are expressions of the official liturgy of the Church. Clearly, baptism is a given and is so revealed in Benedict's central attention on the Paschal Mystery. Easter is the starting point and goal of the monastic year.

The yearly schedule leads to Easter and is derived from Easter. The Eucharist holds a place of honor in the monastery and so also the priesthood, which Benedict honors. Reconciliation, whether considered as a Sacrament or not, is still an important aspect of monastic life, as seen in Benedict's directive for the abbot to recite aloud the "Our Father" in the presence of the praying liturgical community, emphasizing the importance of the words "forgive us as we forgive."

It is clear from the Rule and from life's experience that we need signs, that we need to express what is inside of us, that we need ritual to teach us how to express respect and love and honor. Weddings, funerals, graduations, presidential inaugurations: all have their rituals and liturgies that enable us to in some way make an adequate expression of the meaning of events. They do not say it all, but they give us a way of indicating what is deeply inside of us. It is this recognized need that is inside of us that then becomes the source of liturgical expression, art and poetry and many forms of artistic presentations that have been inherent in monastic life from the beginning.

Art in Monastic Life

The first time I went to Japan I tried to learn at least some of the simple forms of *konji*, or signs, that make up the written language. I kept wishing that, even though they had three sets of what we would term alphabets, they would come up with a strictly phonetic alphabet that would help people like me understand more clearly what the language said. As I came to appreciate more what the language was saying and what the signs were indicating, I began to change my mind about that phonetic alphabet. There is such a richness in the *konji*, the pictographic signs, that a great deal would be lost if the *konji* were to be abandoned.

For instance, those who live according to the *Rule of St. Benedict* take a vow of *conversatio*, which frequently is simply translated as a vow of conversion of life. The word itself, however, is the Latin translation of the Greek *politei*, which has to do with citizenship or belonging. That is not at all as clear to our intelligence as the word for monk would be in Japanese, for instance. On one of my trips to Japan I asked a Soto Buddhist priest friend what the Japanese word would be that would translate the word *conversatio*, or manner of life. I explained to him my understanding of its meaning in English. He came up with the word for monk, which in Japanese is *shudoosha*. The parts of this word came out this way: *shu* means learning, training, struggling or being trained; *doo* means a way of living which is ongoing and continuous; *sha* means a person, man or woman. So a *shudoosha* is a person who is learning or struggling or being trained to live life, or to lead a way of life according to the teachings of a specific teacher. And all of this is expressed in simple *konji* form. This sounds very much like *The Rule of St. Benedict*, where we are told we enter into the school of the Lord's service where we give up our "own will, once and for all, and armed with the strong and noble weapons of obedience . . . do battle for the true King, Christ the Lord."

Whatever the manner of life the follower of Christ chooses or is called to, that life is to make known what it means to put on Christ, to become the revelation of Christ so that through our manner of life people will come to know the God of Jesus. The gospels impress us with the way Jesus lived, a manner of life that was at least as important as the words he spoke. His life was his message, just as married life reveals the mystery of Christ and Church, and monastic life reveals the inclusive love of God for all people. Whatever our manner of living the Christian life, we are meant to be light to the world. This is what we might call the art of monastic life.

The signs we call words contain what we did not plant in them. We inherited a language just as we have inherited all sorts of signs that speak of the reality of life. I have learned a great deal from poetry in this regard. A poet can express a deep reality in simple words, but words that point the way to mystery somewhat enlightened, to a reality beyond the words spoken or written. Poets will speak in metaphor, symbols, similes, and so on. Put them all together and the end product is greater than the sum of its parts. But it still does not exhaust the subject.

For many years I have been an admirer of the Japanese artist Sadao Watanabe. At my abbey we have a collection of his prints.

In my visits to our monastery in Japan I always wanted to meet this man whose biblical scenes and depictions of the saints I have found so attractive. Finally, in the fall of 1995, I had the opportunity to go to his home and have tea with him and his wife.

While we were there, we talked about a work he had done in 1990 depicting St. Benedict. It was while we were talking about this work that he showed us the as-yet-unfinished work he was doing of St. Scholastica, the twin sister of St. Benedict. He explained some of the symbols he had used in this and in the one of St. Benedict, and showed some of the contrasts between the two as well. I was impressed.

It was then that I asked him how he went about producing such a work. It was interesting to know that he made his own paper, created his own colors, and so on. But my main interest was what did he do to prepare himself to produce the work of art. His answer was wonderful.

The monastic superior of our priory in Tokyo at the time was Father Kieran Nolan. Mr. Watanabe was asked by him to do the St. Scholastica depiction just as he had done the one on St. Benedict five years earlier. Mr. Watanabe said that Father Kieran had given him a copy of the *Dialogues* of St. Gregory the Great, which tells the story of Benedict and Scholastica. He told me, "I read it over and over and over again. Then I meditated on it over and over again. Then I did it." I smiled very broadly at his words and told him "That is what we call *lectio divina*." I believe that was the way he did all of his art, most of which was inspired by the sacred scriptures of the Old and New Testaments.

We spent about an hour and a half with Mr. and Mrs. Watanabe that day, and when it came time to leave we went through the common Japanese ritual of bidding farewell. We bowed to each other, one trying to bow lower than the other. Finally, I placed his joined hands between my own, and he knew exactly what I was doing. I honored those hands that had done such magnificent work, hands belonging to a man who had so interiorized the gospel that he communicated to great numbers his own reverence for God's work. Three months later Mr. Watanabe died. I will forever be grateful for the grace of having met him and his wife.

In February of this year, a man by the name of Count Balthazar Klossowski de Rola, otherwise known as the artist Balthus, died at the age of 93. On February 20, 2001, Zenit News Service from Rome published a report on their Internet site on an interview he gave to the French Catholic weekly newspaper, *La Vie*, his last public interview. In that interview he said, "To paint and to pray are the same thing. I have never thought of painting in any way other than as religious activity."

Zenit continued:

> The painter took pains to explain how he lived his artistic inspiration: "A ritual that needs prayer and then silence. When I am in study, it often happens that I cannot paint. I must first sit in front of the canvas, look at it, and caress it with my hand. It is another way of painting, of proceeding. . . . To paint means to reach, to proceed, and to conquer—to go through secrets, translate what is still obscure, and not try to give interpretations. What is important is that the painter himself often does not know the reason. . . . Suffice it for him to have the will to communicate to the world through his darknesses."

One of the greatest modern monastic scholars and writers was Father Jean Leclercq, now deceased, a monk of Clervaux in Luxembourg. In 1980, for the sesquimillennial celebration of the birth of St. Benedict, he made a presentation that was subsequently published in a book entitled *Monasticism and the Arts*. He makes reference to the *Rule of St. Benedict*, chapter 57, "The Artisans of the Monastery," where St. Benedict says:

> If there are artisans in the monastery, they are to practice their craft with all humility, but only with the abbot's permission. If one of them becomes puffed up by his skillfulness in his craft, and feels that he is conferring something on the monastery, he is to be removed from practicing his craft and not allowed to resume it unless, after manifesting his humility, he is so ordered by the abbot.

Father Leclercq says of this:

> There is no sharp distinction between those called "artists" and those we would call "artisans." Both produce works governed not by the spontaneous forces of nature but by the spirit. . . . Under the label "art" are included therefore such activities as writing, spinning, weaving, painting, architecture, and the composition and performance of works of music: in a word, all that goes toward transforming any reality of the material order into a work born of the spirit.[4]

He further explains something of what he sees as the essence of art, and I quote at length:

> The spontaneous comes from nature, but art is born of humans given freedom by God the creator of all to arrange nature's resources in new patterns. In artistic creation there is always embodied the element of choice, of novelty, of the unexpected, and consequently of the wonderful and surprising. Like everything else in humans, subject as they are to sin, this creative capacity can be used for good or evil, to free them from passion or to hold them captive to it. . . . God endows the artist with a wonderful capacity to make his or her own life a work of art, as the artist's nature is refined through asceticism and by developing the gifts bestowed by God. And it is precisely "culture" that enables the artist so to improve upon nature; for the word *culture*, often found in association with the work and names of holy monks and sometimes even with God's name and Christ's, designates all forms of work and *industria*—from agriculture to the knowledge of divine realities and the cult of divine things.[5]

I am not an artist nor a historian of art, monastic or otherwise. Once in my life, when I was stationed in New York, I tried my hand at water colors and one day got so absorbed in what I was doing that I worked on a piece for two hours straight and finally noticed that my radio was not on and I did not have WQXR serenading me as I usually did at free times. That experience alone taught me something of the kind of single-mindedness that prayer and even all of life can become.

Or I remember the time I was truly inspired by a Broadway performance of *Hello Dolly*. The lead was played by Ginger Rogers and when she sang the song, "Hello Dolly," she danced around the apron surrounding the orchestra. At the completion, the whole audience was on its feet cheering, and she did it again—an encore. I do not think I had ever witnessed an encore in the middle of any Broadway performance before or since. When I got home that night all I could think was that as a monk/priest, my involvement in monastic life and liturgy should be as wholehearted as I had witnessed that evening. She was Dolly; I have to be Christ.

So what might the monk become who by faithfulness and dedication perseveres in this school of the Lord's service? And does it make any difference to the monastery itself, to the Church at large, and to all of humanity? I am reminded of a beautiful passage in *Godric*, my favorite book by Frederick Buechner. He says, concerning pilgrims who come to visit the hermit:

> To touch me and to feel my touch they come. To take at my hands whatever of Christ or comfort such hands have. Of their own, my hands have nothing more than any man's and less now at this tottering, lamewit age of mine when most of what I ever had is more than mostly spent. But it's as if my hands are gloves, and in them other hands than mine, and those the ones that folk appear with roods of straw to seek. It's holiness they hunger for, and if by some mad grace it's mine to give, if I've a holy hand inside my hand to touch them with, I'll touch them day and night. Sweet Christ, what other use are idle hermits for?[6]

I entered my monastic community forty-seven years ago and have seen those who entered before me leave feet first after many years of faithfulness to their call. Not all were easy to get along with all the time, but I cannot thank God enough for the examples of struggle and victory that I have seen. I recall Brother Hubert Schneider, accomplished cabinet maker who taught us (at the time) young monks as much about humility as carpentry—and perhaps with as much success. Or Brother Stephen Thell, who created beautiful altar pieces out of wrought iron and taught us the meaning of service to others. Or Fathers Conrad Diekmann and Dunstan Tucker, whose love for Shakespeare and Dante respectively was exceeded only by their genuine and pure love for their confreres.

One of my confreres of late has become a poet and I suspect that one of his poems emerges from his long experience as a monk. Father Kilian McDonnell wrote this poem, entitled "Perfection, Perfection."

I have had it with perfection.
I have packed my bags,
I am out of here.
Gone.

As certain as rain
will make you wet,
perfection will do you in.

It droppeth not as dew
upon the summer grass
to give liberty and green joy.

Perfection straineth out
the quality of mercy,
withers rapture at its birth.

Before the battle is half begun,
cold probity thinks
it can't be won, concedes the war.

I've handed in my notice,
given back my keys,
signed my severance check, I quit.

Hints I could have taken:
Even the perfect chiseled form of
Michelangelo's radiant David,
squints.

The Venus de Milo
has no arms,
the Liberty Bell is
cracked.
                    (June 18, 2000, St. John's Abbey)

It is Father Kilian's poem that has brought me to think of the
way artists have frequently portrayed Christ and other subjects of
sacred art. Scenes of the crucifixion will show the very athletic
and perfect body of Jesus hanging on the cross. Or we see Mary
being visited by the Angel Gabriel at the annunciation, Mary
regally attired and in a splendid palatial setting. Or there is the
Assumption of Mary by El Greco, royally dressed as she rises
above apostles to be greeted by choirs of angels. Often we have
been presented with the perfect as a reminder of the perfection of
the divine and the imperfection of the beholder. Some viewers
have gotten the impression of a goal beyond our reach. Other
artists have presented the suffering Jesus, the sorrowful mother,
the martyred saint in such sad ways as to again make us feel our
inadequacy.

Zenit News Service, on April 12, 2001, published an article
entitled, "How Women Theologians See God," from the book,
How We See God, a collection of writings published by Desclee de
Brouwer publishers. Directed by Isabel Gomez-Acebo, "married
and the mother of six, and a founding member of the Association
of Spanish Women Theologians," this Association is quoted as
saying:

> The principal problem that women have in speaking
> about God is that all the language and categories coined
> have been done by men, from the vantage point of the
> values they regard as sublime: omnipotence, transcendence,
> luminosity, which clashes head-on with the sensitivity of

the weak, where we women are traditionally placed, who see an immanent God sharing the life of suffering.

Further on Ms. Gomez-Acebo said, "We are in the phase in which language categories have not been created that express the God in which many of us women believe. To speak of the weakness and immanence of God, continues to elicit rejection in many circles, despite the fact that our Redeemer died a failure on a cross."

There have been those whose depictions of the sacred capture something of the hope that Paschal spirituality is meant to implant in us. There are the scenes of journey that mean there is a destination to be reached through perseverance. There are the sculptors whose works reveal humanity in very unfinished and rough poses that proclaim: we are not there yet but we are moving. Examples include Doris Caesar's John the Baptist in the baptistery of St. John's Abbey, and Alberto Giacometti and his depictions of people in very rough attire, stark and down-to-the-essentials-looking human beings, but moving forward in hope.

Maybe this is the type of expression in art that is needed today in a world and in a church that knows a lot of imperfection and downright sin. We are not perfectly the Body of Christ yet, we do fail, the evidence is all around us, and we do not have to dishonestly hide our sin. But we will not remain down. We are people of hope.

Monasticism's Contribution

So now the question is: What contribution has monasticism made to the Church and to society in all these years in regard to liturgy and sacraments, *lectio divina*, and art? When we look at the so-called active orders in the Church we find missionary work, preaching, teaching, heroic poverty, availability to serve at a moment's notice in far flung places, and so on. Many of these things monks have done for centuries as well. But here in a monastery is something more essential to our lives, and that is stability in a community where we faithfully serve until death enables us to become the sacrament of the Paschal covenant for all to see who will see.

St. Benedict wanted his monasteries to be known. He recognized that monasteries are never without guests, so he made sure that all who present themselves be received as Christ. It is this hospitality that is a major principle in the life of the monastery. He knew that guests will not be received as Christ unless Christ is preferred by the monk to absolutely everything else. He is to recognize Christ in the abbot also, and in the infirm who are to be taken care of as Christ.

St. Benedict also wanted his monks to live a monastic manner of life, living under a rule and an abbot and being faithful to the monastery until death. The faithfulness of the follower of Christ, whether in the monastery or outside of it, is a revelation of Christ's faithfulness to us. The monk's faithfulness to God and to his fellow monks becomes the image of the law of Christ, "since whoever does not love the brother he can see cannot love God whom he has not seen" (1 John 4:20).

The witness of prayer in community is provided by the very context of monastic life and shows the monk, one another, and the whole world that our God is worth the dedication of a life to the praise of God. This is a witness needed in a world concerned with material gain at the expense of mindfulness of God. This commitment to good liturgy and the sacramental life is a gift to the whole Church, that we might know the difference between mere ritualism and sacred ritual that announces God in the events of salvation history and in the present celebration of the sacred mysteries handed on to us.

Monastic men and women are witnesses to the effectiveness of *lectio divina*, the prayerful reading of the Word of God and those writings that comment on the Word of God. The effect of this *lectio* way of life is the union created between members that provides a visible sign of what it means to be the Body of Christ. And it is this *lectio* way of life that produces the liturgy, the art, and the architecture that one could term sacred because it creates in concrete form the fruit of the contemplative spirit fostered by absorption in the Word of God, the same contemplative spirit in which the total mission of the Church is rooted. And just as the budding fig tree heralding spring is a parable of the signs of the coming of the Lord, so those who genuinely live the Christian life reveal the presence of the Lord, that he is right at the gates.

Monks are no better and no worse than anyone else. Their way of life is an alternative way of saying Christ to the world, just as marriage is a way of saying Christ to the world. Following what St. Paul describes in 1 Corinthians about the gifts of the Spirit, we can say that there are communal charisms as well as individual charisms. Monastic life is one of the wonderful ways God has given us to be witnesses to his life, death, and resurrection, signs of the Paschal Mystery that gives meaning to the Christian life.

Notes

1. Gregory the Great, *Dialogues*, Book II, in *Life and Miracles of St. Benedict*, trans. Odo J. Zimmermann and Benedict R. Avery (Collegeville: The Liturgical Press, 1959), 1f.

2. John Meyendorff, *Byzantine Theology: Historical Trends and Doctrinal Themes* (New York: Fordham University Press, 1990), 13.

3. Edward Schillebeeckx, *Christ, the Sacrament of the Encounter with God* (New York: Sheed and Ward, 1963).

4. Jean Leclercq, *Monasticism and the Arts* (Syracuse: Syracuse University Press, 1984), 69f.

5. Leclerq, *Monasticism and the Arts*, 71.

6. Frederick Buechner, *Godric* (New York: HarperCollins, 1980), 43.

Ways of Encounter

JOHN T. NOONAN, JR.

No one has ever seen God, St. John's gospel assures us, except the Son. Nor, despite the expression "odor of sanctity," has anyone ever smelled God. Taste and see that the Lord is sweet, the Psalmist says, but we do not take the advice literally. Nor can we reach out and touch God. But do we hear God? Karl Rahner has an essay provocatively entitled "Conversations with Silence," the title suggesting that he hears no response to his words of prayer. Speech is the way one person communicates with another person. If God does not speak to us, we are abandoned. I doubt that we converse with silence.

Any modern person hesitates to say God speaks to him. We are aware of how misleading subjective impressions may be. Do we hear God's voice or our mother's? Today we are confronted by militants who claim God's authority for their acts of belligerence. Yet I would have to testify that when attentive to conscience and its guidance and the sense of sin that attends it, I am conscious of listening and of hearing not by my auditory organs, of course; the speech heard is not conveyed by waves of air but is part of an internal dialogue whose source is beyond me.

I am, perhaps, on more objective ground when I recall my encounters with others speaking for God and quoting his words in the context of the Church. Although we do not often attend to it, we hear God in scripture only as he or his representatives are quoted by the sacred writers. There is sometimes an immediacy to the text that impresses us as if we were hearing the words directly from the original speaker. But the Ten Commandments (the Ten Words in the Hebrew) exist in quotation by the Pentateuchal authors. The Sermon on the Mount is quoted by Mark, Matthew,

and Luke. Scripture is the Word of God, but its inspiration does
not convert the text into God's direct speech.

When I first read the words of these messages, I heard them
as the words of God speaking to me. Now I understand that the
Hebrew commandments were portions of the legislation of Israel;
that how they are translated makes a difference (Is it "You shall
not kill" or "You shall not murder"?); that the author or authors
are often pseudonymous; and that the author of Exodus is quoted
by the author of Deuteronomy so that there is at least a double
quotation in the latter's transmission of the basic rules of behavior.
And I realize that the Sermon on the Mount may be a composite and
not a single discourse and that, again here, quotation of a quotation
may occur from a text common to the three evangelists. Sensible
as I am of these imperfections of the medium, I still respond to
their teaching as to the voice of God personally heard.

To turn to one extra-canonical work of great significance to
me since the age of about eleven, *The Imitation of Christ*, by
Thomas à Kempis, here is an author who successfully imperso-
nates God; that is, at times he addresses us as if he were God. For
example: "Son, you are not yet a valiant and prudent lover. The
question, Why Lord? is interjected. God continues: Because on a
little opposition, you fall off from what you have begun." And
the Lord's analysis of spiritual sluggishness goes on for several
pages of chapter VI of Book III of the *Imitation*.

There are parts of the *Imitation* that could be read as *centos*,
composites of scriptural verses, as in the introduction to Book IV:

> Come to me all you who labor and are burdened
> And I will refresh you, says the Lord.
> The bread which I will give
> Is my flesh for the life of the world.

Such passages move from explicit quotation to paraphrase in
which the Lord is presented as the speaker. The employment of
scripture adds authenticity to the speaker's voice. As I read the
above passage, I hear the Lord.

This paper, you will observe, mixes reading and hearing, just
as my account of conscience is not literal but speaks of speech and

hearing that do not depend on tongue or ears. Reluctantly, I am driven to concede that the speaking and the hearing are immaterial and must be metaphorical.

It disturbed Thomas Jefferson that God should be immaterial. For Jefferson, what was immaterial was nothing, almost as for a lawyer what is immaterial is irrelevant and not admissible as evidence. A believer himself, Jefferson contended that God consisted in very fine matter. I sympathize with Jefferson's desire for the tangibility of matter, but I think that he has not understood the terms he is using. A material God would be a finite, physical entity. We might be pleased to touch, taste, smell, see, and hear such an entity, but it would not be God, a being unconfined by space and time.

Communication to and from this spiritual being is, at least normally, spiritual, and that means it must normally be metaphorical. We communicate to God by images derived from our earthly existence. God communicates to us by similar images. God does not have literally a right hand, at which, according to the Creed, the Son sits. The coming Judgment by the Son will not be a judicial proceeding with witnesses, cross-examination, and an address by defense counsel. The physical image of the right hand, just like the social image of a court, functions to convey a reality that by its nature cannot be captured in literal language.

It is thus wonderful but not so surprising that I should encounter God in the Eucharist after its consecration by a priest quoting the words of the Lord, "This is My Body . . . . This is My Blood." Now, preceded by hearing, there is taste and smell, touch and seeing, of the bread and the wine, of course, but understood as a way in which God comes to us. Here is the very tangibility, the materiality, for which Jefferson longed. The symbolic united to the sacramental conveys a reality present beneath the material signs.

The language in which communication occurs is something that has interested me since childhood. My mother told me the story of Eve and the snake. She recalls that my response, at an early age, was, What language did the snake speak? More recently, my friend David Daube, a great student of the New Testament, raised the question of how Jesus and Pilate conversed; Jesus did not speak Latin, and the Roman governor would not have learned Aramaic. Analogously but differently, the sign language used for communication in the Eucharist presents the question of whether a translation is needed. But there is a language in presence that dispenses with words.

In this ever-repeated ritual, in the books I have mentioned, in my inner being, I have encountered God. Let me add a further place that you will recognize by the words spoken: *Ego te absolvo*, as the old rite put it, I absolve you, as modern practice phrases it. Here the priest acting for God performs an act reserved for God: he forgives sins. His act is not psychological counseling, not an exhortation to a better life, not an expression of solidarity in the spiritual journey. The priest's role here is sometimes compared to that of a judge, sometimes to that of a doctor. *Ego te absolvo* are words that neither a judge nor a doctor can speak. Offenses are being forgiven. Only God can forgive them. In three simple words I encounter the Ego who, speaking through the sacerdotal surrogate, is God forgiving.

Prayers and rites and sacred books and the prompting of conscience are, no doubt, only the most formal, the most explicit forms of encounter with God. In a multitude of other ways—in music and painting, as well as in reading; in mountains and oceans, storms and starlight; in teachers and pupils, colleagues and friends, above all in parents and siblings, wife and children—I encounter the providential, the ordered, the gifts that are beyond chance and luck, that are recognizable as manifestations of the Spirit. I could, I suspect, discern a pattern in my life that I could read with devotion as communication from God. I grasp the possibility of such a pattern, I may perceive it, I accept the teaching of Thomas Aquinas that Providence has a plan, and of my friend John Dunne, who says that "things are meant," but I refrain from being certain in my reading of the pattern. In my interpretation, I will stick to encounters with God in the holy books, the holy rites, and in the subjective certainty of conscience.

When did these communications from God begin? I have dated with some confidence my first reading of the *Imitation*. Communion and confession began at the canonical age of seven, but I am now unsure of when I was penetrated by their meaning.

Similarly I heard the gospels read as soon as I was able to attend Mass with my parents, but I find it difficult to date exactly when the words of the Lord began to speak to me. By eleven or twelve, I should guess, I had some sense of God communicating in the ways I've enumerated.

Let me turn to the other side of meeting God, the response side. Of course, the two sides can be separated only for purposes of presentation. One no doubt implies the other. But I speak now of my efforts to communicate. The "Our Father" and "Hail Mary," as well as the story of Adam, Eve, and the articulate snake, I learned from my mother early in life. You know that in one prayer God is located firmly in heaven, addressed only as our common father, and celebrated as exemplary in his treatment of offenses. In the other prayer God, not addressed directly, is presented as a child. Those two prayers I met again as they formed the substance of the rosary. Is it necessary to add that they have been basic to me for about seventy years?

I have sometimes wondered if we should not seek to be original in prayer. Is there not danger in repeating the old formulas? In writing and in public speaking, we value creativity. It is hack work to revise or remodel the words of another; it is plagiarism to copy them. It is parroting to say what someone else has put in your mouth. But in prayer we all say the same old words. Let's grant that stable formulae are the staple of ritual. Why are they a necessity of private prayer?

To these questions, my first response is that the "Our Father" has the authority of its author. No one will improve on the Lord. The "Hail Mary" is in part a *cento* of gospel texts and in part a very old addition to these texts; as a composite, the prayer became popular in Europe as an affirmation of the goodness of procreation in opposition to the Cathar view that procreation was a special sort of disaster. Only the *Salve, Regina* competes with it in expressing devotion to Mary, and nothing equals its simplicity and succinctness. When such a prayer exists, ingenious invention is not needed. And in my experience, for daily use the traditional prayers suffice.

Do I speak for myself when I repeat—quote, as it were—the words of someone else? When I ask such a question, I am reminded that I am in a community. I use the common words to express our joint petitions to our Father and to ask Mary to pray not for me but for us.

These simple prayers, we all know, form a structure when, with the Creed and the Gloria, they become a rosary. Here the repetition of the words subordinates their meaning to the meditation that accompanies them. A kind of double consciousness exists: a consciousness of the recited words, a consciousness of the mysteries commemorated. From time to time, and at some ages more than others, I have reached to the rosary. It is indelibly associated for me with my birth month, October, and with Michelangelo's *Last Judgment*, where the rosary runs down from Mary's lap to the edge of the ledge where sinners may still grasp it and not perish.

I turn from these ways of communicating to God known and used since childhood to the ways provided by the Mass, known and used by me almost as long. From the closely-woven whole, let me single out three passages, as follows:

The Confiteor. A wonderful practical compromise, an acknowledgment of sin without specifications so it is public yet private; a comprehensive acknowledgment not only of deeds but of words and of thoughts, so that sin is seen as more than material; an acknowledgment first to God but then to the community present as well as to that community composed by the saints.

The Offertory. God is asked to grant us by this mystery of water and wine to be co-sharers of the divinity of him who humbled himself to become a partaker of our humanity. Our rise is put in parallel to Christ's incarnation. He became man. We ask to be *consortes*, co-sharers of divinity. Is there any bolder prayer?

The Post-Offertory Prayer. We ask God to give us some part and partnership with the saints, into whose consortium we ask him to admit us. I do not suggest another English word for the Latin consortium, sometimes translated as "company"; the Latin emphasizes the idea of co-sharing. As in the Offertory we ask to be co-sharers of divinity, so afterwards we ask to enter the co-sharing of the saints. This repeated appeal to a common destiny with God transcending our individual lives is afforded by the

Mass, together with its central moment of consecration and its complementary moment of communion.

All of these prayers I came to know through the medium of a missal, a missal so constructed that the English translations ran parallel to the Latin text. I learned to read, to say, to offer the prayers in English and then, after I began to learn Latin, a subject I studied from age ten to age nineteen, I came to know them, if not offer them, in Latin. I cannot help confessing an admiration for the compactness of the Latin, as well as a sense of impoverishment in the disappearance of the Latin, the disappearance of missals, and the obfuscation caused by the singing of pallid hymns at the time of the great prayer to be co-sharers of divinity.

A liturgy more familiar when I was growing up than today was the Benediction of the Blessed Sacrament. The star of that service is the poem-prayer *Pange lingua*, a composition in which Thomas Aquinas showed his truest genius, that of a poet. I do not know any adequate translation into English. I have tried, without great success, to make one myself. Let me only on this occasion offer a literal approximation of it:

> *Verbum caro, panem verum*
> *Verum carnem efficit*

> True bread is made
> True flesh
> By Word-Flesh.

The poetry has the concentration of a haiku. It goes on:

> *Fitque sanguis Christi merum.*
> *Et si sensus deficit,*
> *Ad firmandum cor sincerum*
> *Sola fides sufficit.*

> And pure wine is made
> The blood of Christ.
> If the senses fail,
> Faith alone suffices

To strengthen
A sincere heart.

I have lost the rhythm and the rime. The emphasized tension remains between what is perceived and what is believed. And what is decisive? A heart without guile like Nathaniel's and faith alone. How *fides sola*, faith alone, would echo in another century and another context is irrelevant.

Outside of liturgies and daily prayers, I have found the prayers that run through *The Imitation of Christ* to be inspiriting, even though I have read rather than recited them. To read about a person is not the same as meeting the person, but the reading may excite one's desire to meet. For example, "Invisible God, Creator of the world, How wonderfully You act with us; How sweetly and graciously you dispose with your chosen, To whom You offer your very self to be consumed in sacrament" (I.i.V). The emphasis on the wonder, sweetness, and graciousness of God's action stirs devotion as well as expresses it.

I don't mean to disparage other prayers such as the Psalms (unrivaled in antiquity and range) or the ejaculatory evocation of the Sacred Heart. I speak here only of prayers that have over a long period been measurable means for me to petition, celebrate, or thank God. I need only add that the Act of Contrition must complete this list.

From this selection you can see how much my approaches to God and my sense of encountering God have been set in certain pathways by the pieties that were almost as natural as breathing in what could now be considered the old church, though one not radically different from the new. No doubt there was great attention in my upbringing to the relation of the individual to God, more attention than would be the case today. But, as you also can observe, it was easy to move within the channels constructed by the Church; it was within the community that God spoke and was spoken to.

When speaking of encountering God, one is almost expected to speak of epiphanies, moments when the grandeur of God or the force of his love enveloped one. As you can infer from what I have already said, my encounters with God have mostly been on lines already laid out for me, not special occasions. But I will speak of three times that were special.

In 1947, at the age of twenty, I was doing a post-graduate year at Cambridge University and during the spring vacation visited Capri, Rome, and Lourdes. It was Lourdes that made the greatest impression. The shops selling rosaries and postcards jostled each other like hawkers in a bazaar, but aloof from the sordid commercial scene it generated, the Grotto was unsullied. Worshipers flocked there by the thousand, and were serious, intent, united in prayer. I saw no physical miracle. Lourdes itself, the peaceful assembling of people from all parts of the world, was a moral miracle testifying to the power of God.

Ten years later in the fall of 1957, I was practicing law in Boston and, to tell the truth, bored with the minutiae that make up the day of an associate in a large firm. Dan and Sydney Callahan, then graduate students at Harvard, told me of a wonderful place in Bethlehem, Connecticut, where one could spend a weekend without work or other distractions and find spiritual refreshment. In this way I discovered Regina Laudis, now an abbey, then a priory of a foundation in France. I had never as an adult been on a retreat, and from what I had heard of retreats thought there were too many lectures. At Regina Laudis there were no lectures, only, if one wanted, conversations with Sister Prisca, Mother Jerome, or the prioress, Very Reverend Mother Benedict Duss. Its Benedictine monk co-founder was no longer there, but was reverently remembered. The thread binding the day together was the office sung in choir by the nuns. One could walk, read, meditate as one chose. It was a place for me of spiritual refreshment and reorientation. I came back to it several times in the next three years. Without the experience of responding to God in the context of such a community I do not think I would have been ready to make the most important professional change of my life, to move in 1961 from busily pursuing the business of law to teaching at Notre Dame on a schedule that permitted research in depth on problems in moral theology.

In 1965, still at Notre Dame, I published *Contraception: A History of Its Treatment by the Catholic Theologians and Canonists*, and as a consequence became a consultant to the papal commission on problems of the family. I participated in a number of sessions of the commission in which contraception was freely and fairly discussed. An unanticipated side benefit of being in Rome for the commission was that I was also there for the fourth and final session of the Second Vatican Council. This experience is the third that I mark as special. I have already commemorated it in *The Lustre of Our Country* and draw on that description.[1]

Those of us who had never seen a council—and none of us had—were familiar with the theology that treated as the last word in faith and morals the determinations of a council promulgated with the concurrence of the pope. Pictorial images of councils presented vast and still assemblages of learned males; in some paintings a light shone, or a dove representing the Holy Spirit hovered above the solemn faces. The images were visual embodiments of the pouring out of grace upon the deliberations, which resembled the reception of revelation rather than a parliament of planners.

What we found, in fact, was a legislature in action: a legislature with a right, center, and left; a legislature with a variety of committees composing legislation, compromising disputes, considering amendments; a legislature of bishops guided by staffs of experts; a legislature interacting with the executive power possessed by the pope; a legislature surrounded by lobbyists on every issue.

The conciliar sessions themselves took place in the great basilica of St. Peter, a space suited to the size of the assembly—over two thousand bishops. The side altars of the basilica were turned into coffee bars where over an espresso one could engage in argument with other participants. At the end of each day's session there were press conferences, lunches, cocktail parties, dinners. The work of the Council went on not only in the nave of St. Peter, not only in its coffee bars, but around the town—in religious houses, in hotels, in embassies, in Roman congregations, and in the old palace of the Vatican. The experience of the Council was the experience of a demythologized Church. Those experienced in biblical studies knew that in the documents gathered into scripture God spoke through human tongues in human voices. Now the same phenomenon was observed in the flesh, as it were. The Council was the work of human beings. Faith would accept its conclusions as the will of God. But the conclusions did not come in a disembodied voice from heaven or carved on stone tablets. *Dieu a besoin des hommes* (God needs human beings) a French film of the day was entitled. At Vatican II, I saw how God works through human beings.

In the course of my service on the Court of Appeals for the Ninth Circuit, I have found that, if I deal promptly with each case as it is presented to me, I have time to write on other subjects. I have used that time, for example, to trace in *The Lustre of Our Country* the development and triumph at Vatican II of the doctrine of religious liberty, of the right given by God to human nature and confirmed by the conduct of Christ in proclaiming his message, the right of every person to form his or her religious beliefs free of physical or psychological compulsion. Beyond that kind of exposition, which was at once historical, legal, and theological, I have found solace in composing poetry, largely, though not wholly, unpublished. Permit me to quote from "The Fishwheel," a poem celebrating the ordinary ways of salvation. A fishwheel is a wooden contraption I have seen inserted in the rivers of Alaska as a way of catching salmon. I describe its operation exactly. I use it here metaphorically:

> Anchored to the shore
> By sturdy guy wires
> The fishwheel floats on its log raft
> And creaks rhythmically
> As the strong muddy current turns it.
> The wire baskets on the wheel
> Scoop up the salmon who swim in
> And spin them into the bin
> That is their way station.
> Without water the wheel will not turn.
> Without the wheel the fish will not be caught,
> Without the fish the wheel will be wasted
> And the water rush to no purpose.

The fishwheel is the Church, the fish are us, the water is the grace of God.

Do any of these ways of encountering God prepare one for the encounter following death? I doubt it. Eye has not seen, tongue has not told what is beyond. Metaphors do not bring us there. We do know, retrospectively as it were, that after we were conceived we spent nine moths submerged, unable to imagine the world beyond the womb. Birth was a transformation, and a continuation, of life before birth. Will it be that way after death? So I believe and hope and trust in God who gives me life.

Notes

1. John T. Noonan, Jr., *The Lustre of Our Country* (Berkeley and Los Angeles: University of California Press, 1998).

Simplicity: A Monastic and Christian Ideal

MARIE JULIANNE FARRINGTON

I am happy to be here and grateful and moved. Coming here always feels like coming home. Father Martin asked me to give this talk over a year ago, and I've been thinking on and off about it for several months. In the meantime, the events of September 11 occurred, and that puts us before a terrible dilemma.

I thought I would talk about simplicity when I heard about an interview which Peter Jennings did after September 11 with some of the students of Stuyvesant High School in Manhattan. He was asking them what their impressions were and how these events had affected them, and these youngsters were saying, "My life will never be the same. What I thought was important was to get ahead, to make good grades, to get into the best college, be a success at a great business, and make lots of money. Now that doesn't really matter. It can all be lost in one minute, one second. What matters is life, what you do in life. Every day has to have meaning, helping others, making life better, however you can do that." I sincerely hope that such an attitude will be one of the enduring results of these terrible events.

We have also been told that one cannot just stay with these things, you have to get on with it. I believe that an important part of "getting on with it" is to try to cut to the essential, back to what we might call simplicity. We find very often that limiting situations make faith either grow or diminish. They test us and they can make us simpler. We can hope that what we are going through in the country will lead us in the proper direction.

Simplicity is at the heart of the matter and leads us to what is essential in our lives. We are here partly because we are celebrating the fifty years of Mount Saviour Monastic

Community, and to quote Raymond Panikkar, "Simplicity is the root of monastic spirituality." In his book, *Blessed Simplicity*, he also asserts that the monk is the archetype of the human. In other words, what would be good for the monk, or what would be typical of the monastic life, would also be good for all of us. What the monastic life does is to highlight what the rest of us are looking for and hoping for. Recalling Father Damasus's intentions, simplicity was one of the most important principles of the foundation of Mount Saviour. Simplicity was a principle of reform that Father Damasus saw for the Benedictine life. He insisted, for example, on one class of brother in the monastery. Now that is not so extraordinary, but at the time in which he insisted upon it, it was quite revolutionary. He said that priests would be ordained for the service of the community and worked all his life so that worship would be accessible. He emphasized the contemplative life and believed it would be best, at least for this community, not to have an institutional apostolate, and to be occupied rather with the things of the spirit, the *ora et labora* of the Benedictine life.

There are other expressions of Father Damasus's insistence upon simplicity which are at the root of monastic life. He was seeking an uncluttered life, essential life which would be concentrated on God and on Jesus. And it is true for those of us who are not brothers to say that is what we come here for. We breathe it in, this simplicity and this centeredness; we breathe it in with relief, joy, and gratitude. We feel that after "turning and turning," as the Quaker hymn goes, when we have arrived here we have "come down right."

As far as the Sisters of St. Mary are concerned, our founder was a Cistercian who left his monastery during the French Revolution and its repercussions in Belgium. The Cistercian ideal is simplicity, and that carried over then into the foundation of our community. The biblical word which summarized our spirit is from Chronicles: "In the simplicity of my heart, full of joy, I have offered all to God" (29:17). If you ask a Sister of St. Mary anywhere in the world what she thinks is characteristic of the Sisters of St. Mary, she will say "simplicity," or at least that we are trying to be simple. And so there is an immediate resonance with the spirit of this community and why we have always felt so much at home and nourished by what is lived here.

But what about simplicity? Almost immediately and paradoxically, one comes to the awareness that simplicity is complex, but not complicated. Simplicity has a many-layered richness of reality, or a many-splendored truth. The more one thinks about it and concentrates on it, the further and further one is led in seeing how much is comprehended by simplicity. The few remarks that I am going to make are intended to invite you to think more about it.

In 1948 the Cistercian General Chapter commissioned and approved a document on simplicity. This little book is called *The Spirit of Simplicity: The Characteristic of the Cistercian Order*, and providentially the document arrived at Gethsemane in French. The monastery didn't have many people who could translate, and they gave it to the young Thomas Merton to do the work. When he had translated it, he was a bit dismayed and he felt that the fathers of the chapter had perhaps over-emphasized what was external about simplicity. So he wrote an almost equally long commentary, which is also in the book, anonymously. In this commentary he emphasizes the interior, the internal aspects of simplicity.

There we have one very important pointer: simplicity has to be both external and interior. It has to do with our music, with our clothing, with our food, with all the aspects of our lifestyle, including architecture. This is a constant theme. It has to do, as the Quakers say, with eliminating "cumber" from our lives, those things which weigh us down. After twelve years in Europe, I came back to the U.S. and I admit to being thoroughly ashamed of my cumber. The external expression of simplicity is important and it should not be minimized. It is a part of a whole life, and we must look at it.

To that we must join what we would speak about as interior simplicity.

In a book comprised of the papers from a symposium given by Raymond Panikkar in 1982 on "Blessed Simplicity," he explains his "sutras," teachings for a disciple who cherishes simplicity. Some of them are more evident than others. His first sutra is to allow for "the breakthrough of the primordial aspiration." He means that some place inside of us we long to be simple. More important and evident is the "primacy of being over doing and having." It is more important to be, and more important who we are, than what we have and even what we do. A symposium was held at Mount Saviour in 1992 entitled "Word out of Silence." The word that comes out of silence must be a word that won't hurt, and a true word that builds up.

How do we move forward toward a greater simplicity? The monastic practices invite us to stand daily under the Word of God. Such an invitation asks us to to bring all that we are and have, and the whole world and its history under the Word of God in order to allow ourselves to be sifted and winnowed, refined and defined, by the power of the Word. There is the monastic practice of the *lectio divina*, and in the church, the daily Mass readings. We bring everything into that light and find there a unity, a coming together, a possibility of escaping from a dissipation.

Another of the important ways to simplicity is the experience and practice of silence. Most of us who don't live in the monastery know so little of silence. So much of the talk or the sound in life that we hear is gibberish. Most of us can recognize that place where futile discussions between me and myself go round and round and fill the space of creativity and of growth, the silence where God can be heard. We need so badly to find silence, exterior and interior. In silence, God surely works mysterious wonders.

Another way to simplicity is the practice of "being present where you are." One of Father Damasus's friends and collaborators was Douglas Steere, the Quaker, who has a booklet on being present where you are. Certainly one of the ways to simplicity is to seek to practice being all there, to avoid being divided and distracted, not to be in a drowse of preoccupation about unimportant things. We can be in the same room, we can be in the same life, if you like, and still really not be together, and not have that unity. But simplicity demands a willingness to be vulnerable enough to be influenced by and even to be changed by others. This is what takes place on the deepest levels of love and of friendship, and out of the long loneliness of life, there is a possibility of some luminous moments of profound communion, of truly coming into the presence of the other. There is a simplicity, a unity, that is possible, instead of that separateness, or even conflictual kinds of relationships that we often experience.

Simplicity also has much to do with the capacity for attention. George Washington Carver said, "To see God, look at anything closely." Dag Hammarskjold said, "In the point of rest at the center of our being, we encounter a world where all things are at rest in the same way. Then a tree becomes a mystery, a cloud a revelation, each man a cosmos of whose riches we can only catch glimpses." The life of simplicity opens to us a book in which we never get beyond the first syllable. The capacity for attention is not easily acquired. When we are capable of being attentive, then immediately that sense of separation from others, and from ourselves, and even from our whole world passes. And then we have that wonderful experience that all that is, is one, and that we are united with it. We sense our harmony with the music of the spheres. Perhaps all of our newly emphasized ecological sense ought to be rooted in that kind of simplicity.

Our contemporary challenge, living in simplicity, is not new. It is a problem from time immemorial: the challenge of multiplicity. We need not look far to realize how we are surrounded and immersed in multiplicity. If we consider only the media, and the effect that the media has upon us, or the prevailing philosophies, we find that we are assaulted by a plague of multiplicity and dualism.

How shall we be healed toward greater simplicity and unity? An earlier asceticism would put the accent on elimination and separation from the world. Aspects of that asceticism are certainly valid. However, today's challenge is to find integration. There is a need to cultivate a truly catholic attitude, the attitude that says—"not only, but also." Not only work, but also leisure. Not only heaven, but also earth. Not only woman, but also man. Not only soul, but also body, and so on, in an effort to overcome the dualism that is deeply ingrained in many of us.

The gospel speaks to this question in the story of Martha and Mary, and it is probably not surprising to find that St. Bernard commented again and again on that scripture passage on the question of integration of action and contemplation, doing and listening.

To arrive at simplicity is surely a lifetime's work. One progresses and then realizes that there is a whole lot more to do. While realizing and accepting that fact, it is also terribly important that we realize that we already have a gift, a call, a promise of unity within us. We need to think often of the *shema* Israel: "Listen, O, Israel. The Lord your God is one." And our faith reminds us that each of us is created in the image and the likeness of God. And this unity, which is of the nature of God, is already within us, desiring to be fully realized.

This week I was reading about the death of Isaac Stern, the great violinist. Yo-Yo Ma, Itzhak Perlman, and Michael Wiles, the head of Lincoln Center, were talking about Stern and how he saved Carnegie Hall. Wiles said that the impact Stern had on Carnegie Hall was so immense that he would be a part of everything they do forever. Perlman seconded the thought. "He is leaving a huge void for us," he said. "It's like there will be nobody to take his place, not as a violinist—there are other great violinists—but as a whole personality and force." Father Damasus was like that for me and I think for many other people who knew him. I believe that the unity and simplicity of his personality, and of his being as a human, and as a monk, had been bought at a high price. Once acquired, it certainly engendered an incomparable joy and grace and blessing for those people who met him.

Agape was the core of Father Damasus's teaching and of the monastic ideal, and consequently of the human ideal. Eventually, throughout a lifetime, we should arrive progressively at being the recipient and the mediator of the very agape of God. Our faith teaches us that the Spirit is at work in us, and that our hope is not in vain, to arrive finally at a love without defect or limit, a total, absolute, unconditional love.

Thinking of what is happening in our world, the search for simplicity, the search for the absolute of God, beckons us to find ourselves in the deepest caverns of our own hearts. And there, instead of the implacable hatred of terrorists, we would be able to pose an act of simple, undiluted, undivided love. Doing that would have consequences in terms of the unity of our world, of our being, and of all that is.

Mount Saviour Monastery

A Photographic Record

Joseph Hofbauer in front of the Darmstadt (now St. Gertrude's Guest House) in 1945.

Trimming the vines around the first Chapel, St. Peter's House, 1951.

Original altar and first oratory in St. Peter's the former Hofbauer House), 1951.

The Hofbauer House and present St. Peter's, 1951.

Paul Schretlen and Michael O'Boyle received as postulants, March 4, 1952.

Fr. Placid, Dr. Thomas Boler, Jr., and Fr. Joseph inspecting a cow, 1955.

Our Lady Queen of Peace, August 1956.

Incensing the altar during Eucharistic celebration, 1956.

Monks inspecting one-half of the herd in Spring 1957.

Men dining at noon for the main meal in the monastery refectory in 1958. Men and women guests ate separately.

Fr. Damasus with postulants in front of Casa Litori, 1960.

Frs. Aelred, Basil, and Placid leaving to Christ in the Desert in Abiquiu, New Mexico, 1964.

Sisters of St. Mary of Namur baling the hay, 1970.

Fr. Damasus's funeral, June 30, 1971.

"Word Out of Silence" symposium, August 1972.

Brother Anthony Weber, Brian Tierney, Rozanne Elder, Keith Egan, Fr. Ambrose Wathen, and Carolyn Bynum at a colloquium in 1976.

Arrival of sheep, May 9, 1981.

Mount Saviour's foundation, the Montreal Priory, 1981.

Fall festival.

Oblates Tom Lorenzo, Paul Masolini, Veronica Devlin, Basil Shanahan, and Vince Tolve, with Fr. Martin, October 1986.

Brother Victor with Rhoda Cicotti and her daughter Eliza, tending the lambs in 1986.

A sailboat outing at Lake Keuka in 1991, with Brothers Pierre, Gabriel, and Seraphim, Fathers Martin and James, and Anthony Ciotti.

Summer Program students, 1991.

Monks from Western Priory, Vermont, visiting with the Community of Mount Saviour in 1994.

The Genesee Valley Orchestra and Chorus, directed by Sister Virginia Hogan, SSJ, performing at the Clemens Center with monks from Mount Saviour for the monastery's fiftieth anniversary celebration, May 6, 2001.

Benedictine Peace:
A Meditation on Time

CHARLES DUMONT

Primacy of Eternity

The kind of life chosen by Christian monks—in the world, without being of the world—has long contributed to the moral health of mankind and to the holiness of the Church. This contribution, in part, is due to the gospel way of freedom in which monks see and take time: not as alienating but as the beginning of eternal life. "Your acting should be different from the world's way" so that in all things God may be glorified (*Rule of Benedict* 57; hereafter abbreviated as *RB*). Yearn for everlasting life with holy desire (*RB* 134) and "look forward to holy Easter with joy and spiritual longing" (*RB* 49). Such indications set the earthly direction of the monk. They free him from other desires so that he can "run heart overflowing in the way" (*RB*, Prologue 49) in which "he prefers absolutely nothing to the love of Christ" (*RB* 4), which brings us to everlasting life (*RB* 72, 12). The time of earthly life, then, is like a runway to the take-off.

Eternity in Time

Through the centuries, monks and monasteries have recalled society and the Church to a time beyond time, to the hope of eternal life. It is indeed in time and in one's labor and patience that one advances, badly at first, but then increasingly in faith and time, never losing sight of seeking God, who remains above and before any other concern the preoccupation of the monk.[1] Nothing should become a pretext among passing and earthly things to forget that it is necessary to "seek first of all the kingdom of God" (*RB* 2, 34, 35).

The primacy of the spiritual is found everywhere in the monastic project, but nevertheless it is always and irrevocably linked to the necessities of temporal life. Wise management is required in order that these necessities should lead to liberty of spirit. *Miscens temporibus tempora* (*RB* 2, 24) is a rather enigmatic expression (perhaps derived from a Roman maxim, and found in many languages *a propos* of time): literally: "Fit the time to the times." It indicates that the abbot must adapt to persons and to circumstances. Thus the significance of time will be respected, while simultaneously subordinating it to the reality of eternity. "Day by day remind yourself that you are going to die" (*RB* 4, 47) means, in fact, "put your hope in God" (*RB* 4, 41). When time is related to eternity in this way, the activities of mind and body that fill it are considered as means. And as Kierkegaard has said, means are not distinct from their ends when "eternity penetrates and transcends time." For what is eternal penetrates time and redeems it. To the baptized Christian, all time is composed of favorable moments, since "there is still time to act [so that] by the light of this life, one can do what is useful for Eternal Life" (*RB*, Prologue 43-44). Monks have always wanted to live in a manner freely decided in community that enables them to hasten toward Eternal Life. Within time, the monk has patience as a means of entering the Paschal Mystery, which alone will bring him to his desired end.

The Monastery and Time

All Christian men and woman commit themselves with interior freedom to following Christ. With mature deliberation, the monk makes a profession that he will express this act of love continually and throughout his whole life. It is important to emphasize that by the monk's vows—whose meaning is temporal more than spiritual—God's fidelity is also engaged. The novice prays: "Receive me according to your Word and I shall live; do not disappoint my expectation" (*RB*, Prologue 21). In this prayer, in the presence of all in the Church, the monk openly professes his dependence on divine grace. Eventually, by the action of the

Holy Spirit, the Lord will manifest in his worker, who is purified from vices and sins, the love God has for all humanity in route toward the Kingdom (*RB* 7). Monasteries through the ages, by their bell towers and bells, have continued to awaken us to the mysterious presence of the grace of God in every human conscience that loves life and desires to know happiness. The bells sound a rhythm of time marked by moments of prayer and give meaning to the monk's day.[2]

Community

Through his profession, the monk asks the Lord not to disappoint his expectation. In a spirit of freedom, both interior and exterior, the monk consecrates all of his time to the praise of God and to the expectation of God's coming. The way in which St. Benedict pictures the economy of the monastic life points to the freedom that the monk has in relation to time. Benedict sees time and the monk himself as divine gifts to be dedicated before everything else to give glory to God (*RB* 57). The maxim "time is money" has no more place in the *Rule* than it has in the gospel.

The same freeing disinterestedness governs the way in which monks live community. The conflict of generations is rendered nugatory by the eternal youth of the life of grace. Friendships can be formed, because time in the cloister is not the devouring Kronos of what it produces. Charles de Montalembert, in the great work *The Monks of the West*, best defends this quality of freedom of the medieval monk.[3] As an outstanding representative of Catholic liberalism, he saw in the monastic epoch the essence of the freedom desired for both Church and state. If freedom is the most needed value in our world and in the Church today, it is also the most threatened; so it is good to see how through the centuries monks have protected it, sometimes heroically. In a long introduction, de Montalembert expresses his opinions concerning liberalism, rationalism, and nationalism. He gives us these deeply felt and meaningful lines:

> Their life was carried out and completed in the bosom of
> a hard-working tranquility and sweet uniformity. But it

was prolonged without being saddened. The longevity of the monks has always been remarkable. They knew the art of consoling and sanctifying old age. This, in contrast to modern society where a wholly devouring material activity seems to have become the first condition of happiness and old age is always so sad. In the cloister we see old age not only cherished, honored and listened to by younger men, but so to speak, replaced by that youthfulness of heart which endures through all the snows of age as the prelude of eternal youth.[4]

The Balanced Life of the Monk

The inner peace of each brother of the community, that no one be "troubled or distressed in the house of God," depends on the fact that everything is done in its due time. The same words occur in the *Rule* speaking of the abbot calling for the Divine Office (*RB* 47) and referring to the cellarer giving to the brothers what they need (*RB* 31).

The balanced life of the monk is obviously, first of all, a question of time.[5] The horarium of the day, the liturgical organization of the year, if in close accord with the natural time of night and day and with the seasons, is not a time closed in on itself but one open to the eternal. The ancient city imposed a servitude through its set and exclusive social structure—peasant, artisan, soldier, or "contemplative"—that continued to exist in the Orders of the Middle Ages. But the monastic institution, mainly Benedictine, progressively gave the example of a culture freed from social and political constraints. Among the three monastic works, it is *lectio divina*, the meditative reading of scripture, which occupies an ever-larger place in enlightening and nourishing prayer and work. It unifies life and orients it toward God, while permitting eternity to penetrate time.

In the monastery, the primary intention of the division of temporal activities is the salvation of the soul threatened by lassitude. If the monk does not "have time," that is not the contemporary banal formula that we are always hearing or using. It is because of his poverty, which begins with "his" time, the element essentially linked to his bodiliness, which no longer belongs to him alone (*RB* 33). The favorable time (Kairos) can never be found in the emptiness of agitation or nihilism or in the death-dealing philosophy of the complete idler.

Until the fifteenth century, the mental and spiritual horizon of Christianity was without question an existence given direction by the last ends, where ardent desire for eternal life gave meaning to daily life and to death (*RB* 4, 44-48). The presence of monasteries has preserved and bequeathed this spiritual patrimony, and inscribed it indelibly in history. However it may happen, the Church and her faithful are free to rediscover this vitality. What a historian has written remains true today:

> It is necessary in our time to reconstitute these little Christian societies, mystical bodies in miniature which, in God's time, will become models for the whole of society. These will be Christian families, which for a time, hold within and build up a sense of the meaning of life, judgment on surrounding realities, a scale of values, and respect for conscience. These values are not always appreciated in our time, but through them a better future, preserved and enriched, can be found.[6]

The superior has the responsibility for the wise governance of this church, this miniature mystical body, which draws its life exclusively from the life of Christ. St. Benedict thinks of the superior as a doctor. The superior will always recall the primacy of the spiritual in everyday life. For example, he will shake up the talented artisan who might take his work too seriously (economically or socially). To challenge him, the superior will sell his masterpiece at half price. Is it not God who gives value and meaning to the artisan himself?

The alternating of occupations is obviously salutary to their being well done as the monk is freed from the stress of a specialized result. More important, such alternating relativizes these activities with regard to the eternal. They must always remain means, and must never take on the pretension of being ends in themselves. Rilke expresses this well:

We have never possessed, not for a day,
the clear space in front of us, in which flowers
constantly open. We have the world with us, always,
never that unnamed place which is no place:
the pure, undefined air we breathe and intimately
know and never yearn for.[7]

Isn't this true poverty? Poor persons, recognizing their desire for
the infinite, are often the most available. "Happy the poor of
heart—the Kingdom of God is theirs." If Christianity is
distinguished from other religions by its concern to keep the
temporal within the eternal, it is also true that reality appears only
through the eruption of the eternal into time.

The poet T.S. Eliot perceived the point at which the two
coincide:

Men's curiosity searches past and future
And clings to that dimension. But to apprehend
The point of intersection of the timeless
With time, is an occupation for the saint—
No occupation either, but something given
And taken, in a lifetime's death in love,
Ardour and selflessness and self-surrender.
For most of us, there is only the unattended
Moment, the moment in and out of time,
The distraction fit, lost in a shaft of sunlight,
The wild thyme unseen, or the winter lightning
Or the waterfall, or music heard so deeply
That it is not heard at all, but you are the music
While the music lasts. These are only hints and guesses,
Hints followed by guesses; and the rest
Is prayer, observance, discipline, thought and action.[8]

The monk is at the same time holy and only merely one of
us. With every other Christian, he experiences the continuing
occupation and the "unattended moment" as described by Eliot.
The believer's existence is at once in time and also in eternity.
Angelus Silesius is a spontaneous believer when he declares

"Eternity is so native and profound in us, that willy-nilly we are eternal."

Already, St. Bernard in the twelfth century had said: "Those who enjoy the spiritual peace of their cloisters, by their way of living have already begun to imitate the state of being reserved for them in eternity."[9] Even today visitors to our monasteries often testify to experiencing a kind of timeless peace.

Three Witnesses to the Contribution of Monasticism to the Church and World

In seeking to situate the contribution of monks in the church and world, it is interesting to read what two commentators of the nineteenth century noticed regarding the absence of monastic life in their time. Sören Kierkegaard, who admired the monastic tradition of the Middle Ages, saw monasticism as having the responsibility to recall to the Church that it belongs to two worlds:

> The cloister was, after all, a landmark for determining where one was, that is, if one had advanced toward perfection or had foundered in unadulterated worldliness. The cloisters were allowed to be closed down, and now today we realize that we have been groping foolishly for a good long time in full darkness, trying to find out where we are. The stronghold of the profane has been doing wonderful business. . . .
>
> The more I think about it, the more I come back to this idea; that the religious of the old style—the style of the Middle Ages—that is, the religious of more severe bearing, is an essential element as an intermediary category. Catholicism saw, and correctly, that it was a good thing for this intermediary category to belong as little as possible to the world, and in consequence we find celibacy, poverty, ascesis, etc. . . .
>
> When an individual is rigorously religious and manifests his religious life, people [nowadays] think he is mad. But why? Because the intermediary category is lacking. . . .

There is no doubt that our era, and Protestantism in general, has need of cloisters once more, or at least needs that some should exist. The cloister is a dialectical movement which is essential to Christianity. We need the cloister just as we need a buoy, so we may see where we are."[10]

The second witness is John Cardinal Newman. More fortunate than Kierkegaard, he read the Fathers attentively and discovered there the "monastic system," as he called it. It is in his *Historical Sketches* that we find the story of Anthony. Among long passages which he had translated from the *Life* by Athanasius, Newman inserted comments including these thought-provoking ones:

> It would not be consistent with our present argument to rescue [Anthony] from the imputation of enthusiasm; he must be here considered as an enthusiast, else I cannot make use of him, the very drift of my account of him being to show how enthusiasm is sobered and refined by being submitted to the discipline of the Church, instead of being allowed to run wild externally to it. . . .
>
> If I must choose between fashionable doctrines of one age and of another, certainly I shall prefer that which requires self-denial, and creates hardihood and contempt of the world, to some of the religions now in esteem, which rob faith of all it substance, its grace, its nobleness and its strength, and excuse self-indulgence by the arguments of spiritual pride, self-confidence and security.[11]

These two spiritual masters of the nineteenth century thus stated in well-defined terms the place of monks in the Church, and the need of the Church for them. Their agreement is complete when it comes to giving the characteristics of the monk: simplicity and unity, constituting a quality which Kierkegaard, following tradition, calls "purity of heart."[12]

In his essay, "The Mission of Saint Benedict," Newman comes back constantly to this quality of unity—unity of purpose, of state, and of occupation:

> Simplicity is the temper of children—(or the poet)—and it
> is the temper of monks. . . . From the solitaries of Egypt
> down to the Trappists of this day . . . unity and
> simplicity characterize the monk.[13]

And when monks such as Gregory VII or Saint Bernard were
called to political life at moments of great urgency, Newman tells
us, it was still because the work to which they were summoned
was such that only monks were apt for it, by reason of their
single-mindedness and pertinacity of purpose.[14]

As a final witness, this time of the twentieth century, consider
Thomas Merton. Because of his literary success and the many
connections he had as a result of his spiritual influence, Merton
thought a great deal about the role of monks in the Church. He
suffered all his life from the conflicts of conscience that his
situation brought with it.[15] It was not easy for him to reconcile
the solicitations that came to him from all sides and his own deep-
rooted resolution to remain a solitary. He explained his position
concisely in his article "Openness and Cloister,"[16] repeating that
monasteries should be centers of spiritual life and schools of
prayer. But he was just as adamant about maintaining that the
greatest service, the sole service of monks in the Church, is their
own life of prayer.

In an article entitled "The Contemplative Life and the
Atheist," he writes a commentary on the "Message of
Contemplatives to the Synod of Bishops," of which he was one of
the principal authors:

> Our silence and solitude are not mere luxuries and
> privileges which we have acquired at the Church's
> expense. They are necessary gifts of God to the Church in
> and through us. They are that part of the precious
> inheritance of Christian truth and experience which God
> has confided to us to hold in trust, in order that the spirit
> of prayer and contemplation may continue to exist in the
> whole Church and in the world of our time.
> The laity and clergy who are absorbed in many active
> concerns are unable to give themselves to meditation and

to a deeper study of divine and human things. We feel it is our first duty to preserve for them the reality of a life of deep prayer, silence, and experience of the things of God so that they may not themselves despair, but may be encouraged to continue in their own way to seek intimacy with God in loving faith.[17]

Merton suggested many ways of sharing this treasure: by retreats, works of spirituality, and contacts, either personal or with groups, be they intellectuals, artists, philosophers, or atheists. There might also be meetings of an ecumenical nature, or with contemplatives of non-Christian religious traditions. As Merton noted on another occasion, "Solitude has its own special work: a deepening of awareness that the world needs. A struggle against alienation. True solitude is deeply aware of the world's needs. It does not hold the world at arm's length."[18]

The abrupt and somewhat disdainful contempt for the world that is found in his first works gave way at the end of his life to universal compassion and understanding. He loved to think of himself as a new type of Good Samaritan, himself wounded and fallen into a ditch:

> My monastery is a place where I disappear from the world as an object of interest in order to be everywhere in it by hiddenness and compassion. To exist everywhere, I have to be No-one.[19]

Notes

1. The *Rule* instructs the monks in the following way: "Do not be daunted immediately by fear and run away from the road that leads to salvation. It is bound to be narrow at the outset. But as we grow in this way of life and faith, we shall run on the path of God's commandment our hearts overflowing with the inexpressible delight of love" (*RB* Prologue 45).

2. The sociologist Max Weber has shown that factory sirens, replacing bells, have given another meaning to time, one without any connection to eternity.

3. Count de Montalembert, *Monks of the West* (Boston: Patrick Donahue, Boston, 1872), 41.

4. de Montalembert, *Monks of the West*, lxxvii.

5. See Charles Dumont, "St. Aelred: The Balanced Life of the Monk," *Monastic Studies* 1 (1963): 25-38.

6. Etienne Delaruelle, "St. Benedict," in *Christianity and the Barbarian West* (Paris, 1945), 482.

7. Rainer Marie Rilke, *The Duino Elegies*, trans. Leslie Norris and Alan Keele (Columbia, SC.: Camden House, 1993.)

8. T.S. Eliot, "Dry Salvages," from *The Four Quartets* (New York: Harcourt Brace, 1943).

9. St. Bernard, *Sermons De Diverses*, 84, 2.

10. Sören Kierkegaard, *Journals* (New York: Harper, 1959), X, 298; XI, 532; VII, 152; VIII, 403.

11. John Henry Newman, *Historical Sketches* (London: Baril, Montagu, Pickering, 1876), 103, 125.

12. "Character consists in being one thing. Reason has everywhere done away with character. The infinite has been tidily suppressed. When there is question of the finite, one can hold several offices and be several things at the same time. But on the level of the infinite, man can be but one thing. In other words, to be one single thing is to exist, on the level of the infinite" (Kierkegaard, *Journals*, X, 571).

13. Newman, *Historical Sketches*, III, 2, p. 376

14. Newman, *Historical Sketches*, 381.

15. Charles Dumont, "A Contemplative at the Heart of the World" *Lumen Vitae* 23 (1969): 633-46.

16. Thomas Merton, "Openness and Cloister," *Cistercian Studies* 2 (1967): 312-23.

17. Thomas Merton, *Contemplation in a World of Action* (New York: Doubleday, 1972), 168-69.

18. Thomas Merton, *Confessions of a Guilty Bystander* (New York: Doubleday, 1968), 19.

19. Introduction to the Japanese edition of Thomas Merton, *Seven-Storey Mountain*, trans. Kudo Tadashi (New York: Doubleday, 1966).

Monastic Contributions to Church and World: An Oblate's Reflection

ANTHONY J. CERNERA

I have come to these reflections deeply aware that I am one who has grown up here at Mount Saviour Monastery over the past thirty-three years. I was eighteen years old and a freshman in college when I made my first retreat here. My reflection is as an oblate of this community which means, among other things, that I desire to live the rest of my life in relationship to Mount Saviour.

As I was preparing this paper I realized anew what I have known for years, namely, that I love this place and this community of monks. I also know that I am deeply loved by this community. What an extraordinary gift in my life! How could I ever find the words to give full expression to these bonds of love and to the gratitude that I experience? "How can I repay the Lord for his goodness to me? I will take up the cup of salvation and call upon the name of the Lord" (Psalm 116:12).

How could I respond to the love of God made real for me through my experiences here? The response that has made the most sense to me is to live my life as a disciple of Jesus according to the way of St. Benedict as I have received it and experienced here at Mount Saviour. I desire to live my life as an oblate of this community. In the most ordinary and sometimes in the most extraordinary of ways, I have been formed and reformed here. I have received the grace to fulfill the vocation that God has given to me in a special way through this monastic community.

No one is ever an oblate alone, apart from a community. One is always an oblate of a particular monastery just as the monk is always a monk of a particular Benedictine monastery. We go to God together and God comes to us through the community. So

I am an oblate of this particular place and this particular community, one who belongs to this community and place, at this particular time in history. The Word is made flesh here and now. The paschal mystery is lived and celebrated in this place as it has been for fifty years. For fifty years the monks of Mount Saviour have borne witness by how they live together to the presence and activity of God in our midst. This monastic community is a sacrament of the presence of God in the world. It helps to make visible for all of us that which so often invisible.

As a community, the monks of Mount Saviour give witness to the church and world through the celebration of the Eucharist and of the liturgy of the hours, a common life, and through hospitality to the presence and activity of God in our midst. This is never an easy task, since the Absolute Mystery whom we call God is always an elusive presence. In times of major cultural disruption and upheaval like our own it is even more difficult. In our time what so many appear to experience is not the presence of God but God's profound absence, or indifference to our plight. What an extraordinary vocation and ministry in the life of the Church and for the world it is to live our lives with such a witness in our midst. By seeking God according to the *Rule of St. Benedict*, the monks fulfill a ministry in the church of profound significance and worth. Their seemingly "hidden" vocation has profound social and pastoral implications.

In this paper I will reflect on three themes: the presence and activity of God; our awareness of such presence and activity; the character of monastic witness in today's world.

The Presence and Activity of God

St. Benedict reminds us that we are always in the presence of God, a theme that is constantly illustratedthroughout the Scriptures. As the psalmist cries out: "O Lord, you search me and you know me. You know when I sit and when I stand" (Psalm 139:2). We live our lives in the midst of God in whom we live and move and have our being.

Yet this abiding presence of God is an elusive presence and we can experience that elusiveness as absence. In Psalm 42 we pray:

As the deer longs for streams of water, so my soul longs
for you, O God. My being thirsts for God, the living
God. When can I go and see the face of God? My tears
have been my food day and night, as they ask daily,
"Where is your God?" Those times I recall as I pour out
my soul. When I went in procession with the crowd, I
went with them to the house of God. Amid loud cries of
thanksgiving, with the multitude keeping festival. Why
are you downcast, my soul; why do you groan within
me? Wait for God, whom I shall praise again, my savior
and my God. My soul is downcast within me; therefore
I will remember you from the land of the Jordan and
Hermon, from the land of Mount Mizar. Here deep calls
to deep in the roar of your torrents. All your waves and
breakers sweep over me. At dawn may the LORD bestow
faithful love that I may sing praise through the night,
praise to the God of my life. I say to God, "My rock,
why do you forget me? Why must I go about mourning
with the enemy oppressing me?" It shatters my bones,
when my adversaries reproach me. They say to me daily:
"Where is your God?" Why are you downcast, my soul,
why do you groan within me? Wait for God, whom I
shall praise again, my savior and my God.

The experience of the psalmist is the experience of every one
of us who has sought to enter more deeply into the mystery of
God. The Mighty One who does great things for us is also present
in so many ways that we miss that presence more often than not.

Where is God active? How is God active in our lives? Is there
any guidance from the Scriptures to assist us in understanding the
presence and activity of God in our midst? Let me suggest Exodus
3:1-14 as a possible point of departure. We have here described
Israel's fundamental experience of God. The experience of God is
that of One who is immanent, transparent, and transcendent. The
One who is immanent reveals His desire to be responsive to the
affliction of the Hebrew people and to act on their behalf. But
God commits to freeing the slaves by working through others. God
is committed to the liberation of the oppressed and chooses to act

through others. God is transparent in His actions on behalf of the people. The revelation of God in Moses' encounter with the burning bush also reveals that God is transcendent, beyond the grasp and control of the people. God remains the fundamental and incomprehensible Mystery in the midst of the people.

The Christian community's encounter with God both radically incorporates Israel's fundamental experience and opens us to a deeper and fuller revelation of the Incomprehensible Mystery whom we call God. The disciples of Jesus also came to know God as immanent, transparent, and transcendent. However, this revelation of God invites us into the reality of the Trinitarian Love which is beyond our wildest imaginations of who God is.

The Crucified One whom these first Christians came to know as the Risen One was the Anointed One of God. He is one like us in all things. Jesus was truly human, yet a human who so pushed the dimensions of what it meant to be human—one who was so receptive to the reality of God—that God was indeed incarnate in Jesus of Nazareth. The Word became flesh and dwelt among us. God is immanent in our midst.

Yet the Christian community's experience of God's presence and activity also invited the disciples of Jesus to acknowledge that the Spirit of God was the first gift of the Paschal Mystery. They recognized with the experience of the Pentecost that this Holy Spirit not only dwelt in their hearts and in the life of the community but is also the One who breaths where he wills, moving and shaping the whole direction of history, indeed all of creation. Thus they also experienced God working through them, in their midst, beyond their community as the transparent One.

Yet the immanence of God and the transparency of God did not exhaust their experience of God. God was also always gracious mystery in their midst. Abba! My dear own Father! Gracious, loving, abiding, yet fundamentally beyond their grasp and control. Thus God was also experienced as ever-mysterious, always beyond, even while in our midst. He is the One in whose presence we must take off our shoes and be silent, listening in awe and wonder, in praise and thanksgiving.

For all of the images and metaphors and symbols that the community used to express their experience of God's presence and activity, there emerged one that was the least insufficient. It is from St. John: God is love. God is *agape*, love unconditional, total and forever giving. God is *agape*. The Father gives himself completely to the Son and the Son gives Himself back completely to the Father. Their unconditional love for each other is the Holy Spirit. The eternal communion that is God's inner life is *agape*. The eternal presence and activity of God is love, love made visible in Jesus Christ, finally and most fully on the cross. The immanent, transcendent, and transparent One in our midst is present and active as love. The Word that God speaks is love, the action that God does in the world is love, and the being in whom we live and move and have our being is love. God who is ever-mysterious and beyond our comprehension; always calling life out of death; always calling good out of evil; always inviting us to live in that love and to be that love to one another. God is always laboring to bring creation to its fulfillment in love, so that God may be all in all.

The Human Condition:
Our Blindness Regarding God's Presence and Activity

Among the truths about our existence as human beings that the Scriptures teach us is that we are often blind to the presence and activity of God in our lives. Not only are we blind to that Presence we are also often indifferent and prefer other gods. Yet immersed as we are in this reality, we miss it, we forget it, we tend to live as though it was otherwise. We are blind and often uninterested in the saving presence and activity of God in our midst.

In addition to what the Scriptures tell us we are also faced with factors within our contemporary American culture that plunge us even more deeply into unawareness of the presence and the activity of God.

Let me identify several. First, we live in a world undergoing a profound transformation. Our times are one of those epoch-making moments in history, like the emergence of agriculture or the Industrial Revolution. The scientific-technological revolution, of which we are in the midst, has presented us with changes so profound that most of us do not even begin to comprehend them. However, we know in our hearts—in those quiet moments of reflection—that there is a fundamental shift occurring in humanity's self-understanding. Epoch-making moments like this provide the human community with the opportunity to make a quantum leap in its evolution. However, this shift has also caused us to experience a fundamental dislocation, a hermeneutical dysfunction. For many of us the old language to explain life does not work anymore. We have yet to create a new language to explain our experience. The old metaphors are no longer adequate, and we are in search of new ones as part of our quest to understand our place in the universe. Being in the midst of birthpangs is not easy.

Second, in addition to this profound and often baffling sense of change, there is the emergence of what has been called an excessive individualism in American society. We live in a society that cherishes the right of people to choose for themselves. We take it as axiomatic, as one of the uncritically accepted assumptions of our world, that each of us should choose his or her own pattern of life or lifestyle. This sense of the self as individual was won in no small part by our freeing ourselves from older moral horizons. In the past, people saw themselves as part of something larger. In some cases, this was a cosmic order, a "Great Chain of Being." In such an order human beings figured in their appropriate place along with the archangels, cherubim, and seraphim, and other angels as well as other earthly creatures. This hierarchy was reflected in the hierarchies of human society. Many people were often locked into a given place, a role or a station in life that was properly theirs and from which it was virtually impossible to imagine deviating.

In his important work, *The Ethics of Authenticity*, Charles Taylor writes that the older moral horizons,

> gave meaning to the world and to the activities of social life. The things that surround us were not just potential raw materials or instruments for our projects, but they had the significance given them by their place in the chain of being. The eagle was not just another bird, but king of

the whole domain of animal life. By the same token, the rituals and norms of society had more than merely instrumental significance. The discrediting of these orders has been called the "disenchantment" of the world. With it, things lost some of their magic.

This loss of purpose was linked to a narrowing. People lost the broader vision because they focused on their individual lives. Many seem too often to have lost the sense of being part of a larger whole and of finding our identity in communion with one another.[1]

The third factor that keeps us from an awareness of the presence of God is the triumph of instrumental reason in American society. By "instrumental reason" I mean that kind of rationality we draw on when we calculate the most economical application of means to a given end. The measure of success for us is maximum efficiency, the best cost-output ratio. Let me quote Taylor once again:

No doubt sweeping away the old orders has immensely widened the scope of instrumental reason. Once society no longer has a sacred structure, once social arrangements and modes of action are no longer grounded in the order of things or the will of God, they are in a sense up for grabs. They can be redesigned with their consequences for the happiness and well-being of individuals as our goal. The yardstick that henceforth applies is that of instrumental reason. Similarly, once the creatures that surround us lose the significance that accrued to their place in the chain of being, they are open to being treated as raw materials or instruments for our projects.[2]

Fourth, in today's America we have not only pushed God to the side, we have forgotten about God's cherished ones, the poor and the needy. We live in a world in which millions of children are hungry and hundreds of thousands of them die of malnutrition. This occurs in a world that has the capacity to feed all of its children. We can. We just haven't. Today in the United States one out of every five children lives in poverty. The poor and the needy have become the forgotten people of our society, blamed more often than not for their condition.

Fifth, what results from much of what I have suggested above is the loss of a sense of the meaning and purpose of life. In the face of rampant instrumental reason and excessive individualism, there is an eclipse of concern about our end or goal as human beings. Abraham Heschel pointed this out in his book *Who Is Man?*

> One of the most frightening prospects we must face is that this earth may be populated by a race of beings which though belonging to the race of homo sapiens according to biology will be devoid of the qualities by which man is spiritually distinguished from the rest of organic creatures. To be human, we must know what being human means, how to acquire it, how to preserve it.[3]

E.F. Schumacher described an awareness of our loss of purpose this way:

> After all, everything we do and talk about should be orientated to, and derived from, an answer to the question, "Why are we here in the world anyhow?" We are not using the facilities the Creator has put at our disposal for the purpose of attaining our end. We don't even think about what our end is. We're using things only because they're there. Our engineers and scientists produce something more we could use, so we must use it. We do things because it's possible to do them. We're a society that's rich in means and poor in purpose.

These elements within our culture foster a kind of communal blindness. Human beings are made for communion with God and with one another. We are not isolated egos but beings who find life in relationships with God, with other human beings, with the earth and the universe. Our challenge is to bring people back to this fundamental truth about our human existence. We are blind, and we need sight. We have been invited to the feast but have lost interest. We need once again to rediscover the source of the invitation planted in the very soil of our being. In so doing, we will recapture the passion for the goal of our existence, and we will have a compass for human action in the world.

This is why the monastic witness that this community, and many others like it, give each day is so critically important. By living the life that they faithfully live each day, they offer others a map for the journey of living. Let me suggest some signposts on the journey that they witness to each day.

First, in a society increasingly obsessed with consumerism and materialism, the Gospel lived here according to the *Rule of St. Benedict* teaches that to be human is of infinite worth and value not because of what one possesses but because each person is an image of God. Every human being is a spiritual creature. From the opening pages of Genesis, we learn that human beings were given life when they received the breath of the Lord. The breath of the Lord gives life by dwelling in us. God is the life-giving presence and as such God lives in us. We are capable of possessing the presence of God and even more of knowing God. As spiritual creatures, we are listeners to God's word in history. But there is more to our identity than this. There is in the depths of my being—of your being—the in-dwelling presence of the Holy Trinity. Each of us is an image of God because of the original presence of God in the depths of our heart. This necessarily challenges us to ask, "Who is this God in whose image we are made?"

The second signpost on the road is the affirmation of the principle of the common good. Such a principle affirms creative activity as more important than profit, people more important than things; and it seeks patterns of work that liberate and enhance the human spirit. It is a rich concept in the Catholic tradition and one that needs to be further understood and developed. It is imperative that we experiment with forms of community to give expression to this principle of the common good.

The third signpost on the Christian journey is that human beings are made for communion with God and with one another in the company of the saints. The goal is not the isolated existence of my ego over and against yours, but communion. We are made for communion with God. As Christians, we know that this God is the Father who loves us and calls each one of us by name through His Son in the Holy Spirit. The Incomprehensible Mystery whom we call God is the Triune One who is love and who calls us to communion with Himself and with one another. This communion comes about through love—the love made visible to us in Jesus of Nazareth. This communion which is the goal of our existence is already a reality. It is the original fact of our existence, the forgotten fact but nevertheless the fact of our existence. For us to be obedient is to live life according to this fact of our existence, and is the root of the call to holiness and wholeness. The call of Micah to act justly, love tenderly, and walk humbly with our God is a call to live out this communion. This is my truest self.

When I reach out to the other person, to God, in love, fidelity, and commitment, I become more myself than I was before. The simple yet essential law of our being is that we find ourselves only by giving ourselves away. "Unless the grain of wheat dies," "Love one another as I have loved you," and "Though he was in the form of God, he did not cling to his equality with God but emptied himself" are all insights from Scripture that call us to selfless giving.

The fourth signpost for Christians has two dimensions that are intrinsically connected: remembering the past and radical openness to the future. Our journey to human fulfillment requires that we remember and celebrate the past and also affirm and embody the future toward which we are traveling.

Remembering and dreaming are critical human activities. This is especially true when they are shared in story. This is why the liturgy of the hours and especially the Eucharist are so important to Christians on their journey. The monks' gathering day in and day out for the celebration of the Divine Office and the Eucharist bears witness to this truth. We are a sacramental people who celebrate what God has done and what God is doing.

The fifth signpost is the acceptance of our finitude and creatureliness. In the presence of God, we celebrate our dependence and interdependence. We are nothing without God. But because we have been called into life by the Incomprehensible Mystery, we know ourselves as an integral part of creation who have a special responsibility to bring all of creation to God. In the face of death, we affirm the goodness of life and that with death life is changed, not ended, indeed it is brought to its fullness.

The Character of Monastic Witness

If what I have said thus far is true, then it is clear that monastic witness to the presence and activity of God in our midst is critical. In a world that so easily forgets God, the monastic witness calls us back to the truth about God and about ourselves.

Let me conclude by reflecting on how this witness is made manifest. Like all things Benedictine it becomes apparent in the simple and ordinary things that are done each and every day, which in itself points to a profound truth about God's salvific presence and activity in our midst. This monastic witness is prophetic, contemplative, compassionate, and communal.

Prophetic

Since the Church lives in a society that is essentially drawing its values from a source other than the Judeo-Christian tradition, monastic communities by the way they live embody the prophetic tradition of the Hebrew Bible and Jesus of Nazareth.

The biblical prophet is one who is called by God to be immersed deeply in the Word of God as it is contained in Scripture and is also deeply attentive to the Word of God present in history, in the contemporary world. The biblical prophet is one who listens deeply to dialogue of the Word of God embodied in the tradition of God's people with the Word that God is speaking in the signs of the times. She or he is called upon to speak a word from God that emerges from this great dialogue. Such a prophetic person can assist his or her community in understanding better who it is and what it is called to do. The community's sense of mission in its current historical context emerges as it attends to the task of fidelity to its original call as well as to the present call of the Lord that is heard in contemporary circumstances and events.

Contemplative

Since we live in a society that has lost its way and is, in many ways, without hope about its future, leaders of monastics are called to be contemplatives in the midst of their own busy lives. As Christians, we are invited to discover deep within our hearts the voice of the Spirit of God and attend to the task of listening to what the Spirit has to say. From this important spiritual discipline will emerge the ability to see the world in a different way, to attend to how the Holy Spirit is leading the world toward its fulfillment in the Kingdom of God. It is a basic conviction of the Christian proclamation that the Spirit of God is active in the daily events of our world and is leading it to a new creation. Monastics have the task of discerning the first lines of the revelation of the new world behind the veil of everyday life. Monastics, as contemplative critics, have the task to remind their fellow travelers and pilgrims about the beauty of each human being and of God's creation.

At a fundamental level, it is not our task to go around anxiously trying to redeem people, to save ourselves or the world. We have been redeemed once and for all by God in Jesus Christ through the power of the Holy Spirit. Monastics are called in a special way to help us affirm this good news, and to make visible in daily events the fact that behind the brokenness and pain seen in the tangible things of life, there is something great to be seen: The face of Him in whose image we are shaped. As contemplatives, monastics are immersed in the vision of the new creation that God intends for His creation. Our vision of the fulfillment of human life is rooted in the concrete reality of the resurrection of the One who was crucified and raised from the dead. Through the daily discipline of contemplative prayer, we are developing the sensibility to see the small mustard seed and to trust that "when it has grown, it is the biggest shrub of all and becomes the tree so that the birds of the air come and shelter in its branches" (Mark 4:32).

Compassionate

The monastic gives witness to the saving presence of God by being compassionate, to embodying in his or her life the compassion of God that was incarnated in Jesus of Nazareth. Jesus not only said, "Be compassionate as your Father is compassionate," but he was also the concrete embodiment of this divine compassion in our world. Jesus' response to people in need—the sick, the blind, the lepers, the hungry, the ignorant, the widows, indeed all those who suffer—flowed from the divine compassion which led God to become one of us. Of the many stories in the Gospels showing Jesus' compassion, I am very fond of the one at the end of the first chapter of Mark's Gospel: a leper came running up to Jesus and said, "Master, if you want to, you can cure me." This statement of faith is responded to by Jesus with the words, "Of course, I want to. Be healed." "Of course, I want to?" Jesus is moved with deep compassion.

Twelve times in the Gospels we find a beautiful reference that is attributed only to Jesus and his Father. The expression is "to be moved with compassion." The Greek verb *splangchnizomai* reveals just how deep this goes. The *splangchna* are the entrails of the body. We would say the "guts." They are the place where our most intimate and powerful emotions are located. When the Gospels speak about Jesus being moved with compassion, they mean that he is being moved from the depths of his being. This is nothing superficial or passing. Rather it comes from the depths, from the most intimate and vulnerable part of his being. It is related to the Hebrew word for compassion, *Rachamim*, which refers to the womb of Yahweh. It is there in the womb of Yahweh that divine tenderness and gentleness have their source. When Jesus was moved with compassion, what was revealed was the inexhaustible, unfathomable tenderness of God.

When Jesus saw the crowd harassed and dejected like sheep without a shepherd, he felt with them from the center of his being (Matthew 9:36). When he saw the deaf, the paralyzed, the blind being brought to him from all directions, he willingly opened his heart to them and entered into their pain and suffering. So it was with the widow of Naim, who was burying her son, or the rich man whose daughter was dying. He identified himself with the suffering one. He stood in their shoes and was willing to suffer with them. He was compassionate. Jesus freely and fully enters into our pain and suffering so as to liberate us.

This is what we mean when we say that Jesus reveals God's solidarity with us. In and through Jesus Christ, we know that God is our God, a God who has experienced our brokenness, who in the words of St. Paul "became sin for us" (2 Corinthians 5:21).

The parable of the Good Samaritan (Luke 10:31-36) suggests to us what this compassion is all about. Each of us is familiar with the details of the story from our childhood days. As you recall, all three passersby—the priest, the Levite, and the Samaritan—"see" the victim who is lying by the side of the road. He is stripped of his possessions, including his clothing, and is thus without any visible sign of nationality or social status. The priest and the Levite only "see" the injured man, whereas the Samaritan "sees and has compassion." Compassion is the vehicle for moving beyond just seeing the victims of injustice and violence in our society. Compassion invites us to enter their world with mercy and care. It is a call to stand in solidarity with those who are suffering.

Compassion enables us to enter into the world of other human beings who are in need and to share deeply in their sufferings. But it does not stop there. Because compassion is a divine quality, it challenges us not only to enter into the world of the needy but to leave it in such a way that we have played our part in giving our neighbors freedom. The Samaritan of our parable not only took care of the injured person, he also brought him to an inn, paid the innkeeper the equivalent of two days' wages, and entered into a contract to pay the other bills the injured man might incur. Since the injured man had been deprived of all his resources, he could have been enslaved until his debt was paid to the innkeeper (Matthew 18:23-35). The Samaritan ensured his freedom and independence.

God asks nothing less of us than that we become the compassion of God in the world today, that we carry on the mission of Jesus in today's world.

Communal: Companions With One Another

Since we live in a society where so many of us experience our existence as isolated from others, as bereft of solidarity and intimacy, I believe that another critical characteristic of the monastic witness is that she or he be a companion, inviting others to be companions to one another on the journey of life. To be a companion means to be willing to break bread with the other and to affirm a fundamental solidarity with any human being who is genuinely seeking to live life humanly.

The Gospel of Mark presents the story of Jesus' calling of the apostles this way: "So they came to him and he appointed twelve; they were to be his *companions* and to be sent out to preach, with power to cast out devils" (Mark 3:13-14). First, they were called to be his companions and companions to one another. Then they were sent out to preach and to cast out demons.

A fundamental task for us as leaders is to bring people together, breaking down the walls that separate us; inviting others to the common table where our story is shared, our hope celebrated, and our isolation overcome.

Our companionship is to be rooted in genuine love for the other, a love in which God is present. There is an old rabbinic story that captures this truth:

> Time before time, when the world was young, two brothers shared a field and a mill, each night dividing evenly the grain they had ground together during the day. One brother lived alone; the other had a wife and a large family. Now the single brother thought to himself one day, "It isn't really fair that we divide the grain evenly. I have only myself to care for, but my brother has his children to feed." So each night he secretly took some of his grain to his brother's granary to make sure that he was never without.
>
> But the married brother said to himself one day, "It isn't really fair that we divide the grain evenly, because I have children to provide for me in my old age, but my brother has no one. What will he do when he is old?" So every night he secretly took some of *his* grain to his brother's granary. As a result, both of them always found their supply of grain mysteriously replenished each morning.

Then one night they met each other halfway between their two houses, suddenly realized what had been happening, and embraced each other in love. The story is that God witnessed their meeting and proclaimed, "This is a holy place—a place of love—and here it is that my temple shall be built." And so it was. The holy place, where God is made known to people, is the place where human beings discover each other in love.

Notes

1. Charles Taylor, *The Ethics of Authenticity* (Cambridge, MA: Harvard University Press, 1992), 3.

2. Taylor, *The Ethics of Authenticity*, 6.

3. Abraham Heschel, *Who Is Man?* (New York: Doubleday, 1972), 12.

Ruminations on the Life of St. Benedict

FRANK T. GRISWOLD

I n this essay I am going to do a number of things. I am going to be autobiographical but I am also going to ruminate, to use an ancient monastic term: ruminate upon the life of St. Benedict and the *Rule* that he produced that has guided me over the last thirty-seven years of visits and retreats here at Mount Saviour.

I came first in 1964, at the age of twenty-seven, having been ordained a priest for hardly a year, and I became an oblate of the community in 1968. That is a very precious relationship that has sustained me through the various turnings of my life, that have taken me from parish to parish and then to the Diocese of Chicago, and now taken me to the office of Presiding Bishop and Primate of the Episcopal Church.

Let me begin by drawing from the wisdom of a contemporary monastic, Matthew Kelty, a monk of Gethsemane, who says that the monastic life is essentially a search for reality. The paradox is that from the outside it often seems so unreal, with its costumes, its customs, its patterns of life that can appear exotic and removed from reality as we know it. I have known religious communities intimately since the age of fifteen, when I was sent away by the boarding school chaplain for spiritual direction at the hands of an Anglican monastic in Cambridge, Massachusetts, and I continued to know that community intimately through my university years. As a priest I have given retreats and spiritual direction to religious, heard their confessions, and served as Episcopal visitor to a community of women and a community of men. As such I've been privy to the intimate joys and struggles, the failures, and the victories that have marked the lives of these men and women. I've shared the anxieties of superiors, resolved conflicts, dealt with untoward behavior, celebrated moments of grace and fidelity, and labored with my monastic brothers and sisters to discern in various contexts the shape of their future.

What has impressed me and strengthened me along the way through these various relationships has not been the perfection of the men and women I have shared community with but rather their persistence. That is the thing I think is so important: the persistence of those who perceive themselves called to the religious life. I say all this because it is so easy to be romantic about the religious life. You find your favorite monastery and they sing beautiful psalms. You come and bask in it all and the human struggles and all the stresses and strains are offstage. You only see one dimension of it, and the cost of persistence doesn't really get revealed in the outward manifestations that we so often see. That is why I mention my own associations, because there is actually nothing romantic about my respect and affection for those who espouse the religious life. Their heroism is very real to me, not because they avoid things but because they face things.

Paul, in the fifth chapter of the letter of the Romans, says that "suffering produces endurance and endurance produces character and character produces hope and hope does not disappoint us because God's love has been poured into our hearts through the Holy Spirit that has been given to us." The suffering here is the suffering that happens when we are conformed to the Paschal mystery. The pattern of dying and rising, which becomes the truth of our lives by virtue of our baptism, is lived in a very deliberate way by those called to the religious life. It doesn't mean a kind of masochism, but it means facing into things and being dislocated, in terms of one's own inherited realities. It means being disillusioned, which is very positive because it means illusions and untruth are taken away from us. It means confronting our poverty, being cracked open, as it were, by the Paschal mystery. It means coming to terms with ourselves—our actual selves—which are the sum total of all that we have lived, including wounds and scars that we carry with us. It means embracing that actual self and being disabused of the idealized self that we so often create for ourselves to offset who we actually are. We seek to structure the person we would like to be and struggle to become that person, but it isn't necessarily who God is calling us to be. And so in embracing the actual self—who we really are in terms of the life we have led—and allowing the ideal self, which is an illusion, to be shattered and overturned, we open the way to what we might call the real self: the real self, which is the product of grace working in us and not our own self-construction.

I think here of the apostle Paul, who clearly had a self-constructed piety; he's very forthright about that in the letter to the Galatians. He talks about outstripping his contemporaries in his own religious observance. I think he was trying to offset what he later describes as "the thorn in his flesh." But no amount of self-constructed piety could deliver him from that source of shame and embarrassment, that source of being burdened and incomplete and imperfect. And so, after his conversion he prays to the risen Christ "take this away from me." He prays three times, we are told. And Christ's reply is, "No, my grace is sufficient for you, for my power is made perfect in weakness."

And so it is as we enter into the Paschal mystery—either by virtue of the life we lead as baptized members of Christ's body, or as monastics, which is another form of living the baptismal mystery—we have to confront our poverty. Ultimately, we have to be taken apart. We have to be turned inside out and we discover that dying and rising, losing and finding, being poor and yet rich are the paradox that doesn't make logical sense, but it makes existential and personal sense as grace embraces us and conforms us to the pattern of Christ.

I have seen many a novice and postulant trying to be the "ideal" monastic: often judgmental of the senior members of the community for their seeming laxity, or in most cases their obvious humanity. And I've seen them maintain that posture for awhile, often with great strain, until suddenly they collapse and everything falls apart, often in some very humiliating way. They have a temper fit in the middle of the refectory, or throw food, or do something untoward and they are embarrassed and furious with themselves for having transgressed this ideal self they've been trying to create and live. But that is really a moment of truth. It is where grace can begin the costly and excruciatingly specific work of transformation. It is where reality can grasp them as

Christ in the icon in front of the altar grasps the wrists of Adam and Eve and yanks them out of their coffins, their old constructions, into the new life of the resurrection. And resurrection is sometimes experienced in a painful way because it's not easy or pleasant to be yanked out of our stuckness or our limitations or our idealized selves and pulled into reality.

I am struck by two things that Benedict says at the end of chapter four in the *Rule*, the chapter that deals with the tools for good works, which is a catalogue of right behaviors and attitudes that could be used to reinforce notions of an ideal monastic self. He says, "Place your hope in God alone," and I think he means here place your hope in God's love alone. Even more important, he says finally, "Never lose hope in God's mercy," meaning simply that as you try to live this catalogue of goodness and you fail miserably, instead of descending into self-castigation, open yourself to the love of God, the compassion of God, the enlivening mercy of God.

I think here of Julian of Norwich, that very wise woman of the fifteenth century who said, "In our sight we cannot stand, in God's sight we cannot fall. As I see it," she continues (imagine the authority of saying "as I see it"), "both are true but the greater truth belongs to God." We often see ourselves only as fallen, and God, in God's love for us, sees us as standing. And so part of growing into the authentic self is to make some room for that love of God which always seeks to embrace us and raise us up. Now let me say a word or two about how I first came to Mount Saviour. I came here in 1964 at the invitation of a Roman Catholic priest of the Archdiocese of Philadelphia by the name of Thomas Lawler. He knew something of my interest in the liturgical movement and monasticism, and he said to me, "Mount Saviour is just the place for you." I had no idea what he meant, but I accepted his invitation. And so, in May of that year I came on retreat with a group of newly-ordained Roman Catholic priests from the Archdiocese of Philadelphia. I believe that Tom Lawler had picked each one of us deliberately. We were all assistants or curates in some fashion having difficult times with senior pastors whose views of the Church were clearly out of sync with reality. And we had the answers; we knew just what the Church should do and what the Church should become, albeit in its Anglican or Roman Catholic forms.

That first retreat was an overwhelming experience. Father Damasus gave two conferences each day and I was mesmerized by the breadth and depth of his ruminations. Father Martin, at that point, was the guest master. I remember one day Father Damasus reading to us from the Book of Revelation. He said, "Now listen very carefully, gentlemen." (Probably for members of the community this is a very familiar passage because I am sure he didn't simply use it with a group of newly ordained clergy.) Christ addresses the church at Ephesus, or rather the angel of the church of Ephesus, saying, "I know your works, your toil and patient endurance." And we thought of ourselves patiently enduring idiotic pastors with limited views. "I know that you cannot tolerate evildoers, you have tested those who claim to be apostles but are not and have found them to be false. I also know that you are enduring patiently and bearing up for the sake of my name and that you have not grown weary." And we said, "Yes, yes, yes, that's us." Then he paused and a slightly unholy smile played across his face and he went on with the next verse. "But I have this against you, you have abandoned your first love." And with that he shut the Bible and said firmly, "Gentlemen, never become technicians of the sacred. Always live the mystery deeply and personally or your priesthood will be shallow and your ministrations threadbare." Those aren't exactly his words. I don't think he would have said threadbare, but anyhow, that is the gist of what he said. At that, I was convicted, as I think all of us were, and I have never forgotten that particular moment. I go back to it again and again.

I've used the same text both with priests, when I was a diocesan bishop, and with bishops when they've gathered together, to reflect on Episcopal ministry. In all instances, the text calls us back to a deep living of the Paschal mystery lest we become superficial and external and products of what Father Damasus called the *"église mécanique,"* the mechanical church. In any event that was a life-changing experience.

In addition to the wonderful contemplative liturgy and the celebration of the Hours that drew us all in and opened the psalmody and the scripture to us in new ways, I remember one afternoon Father Damasus saying, "Franciskus, come we take a walk"—sort of a declaration—so we headed off across the field to the west of the chapel. In those days clergy on retreat wore cassocks and I was in my snappy Anglican cassock made by Whipples of London, which doesn't have buttons down the front and is double-breasted. People would look at it and say, "What order do you belong to?" At one point I said "I'm an Anglican." They said, "We've never heard of the Anglican fathers." I realized that I needed to be more specific.

But in any event, I was honored to be invited to take a walk and as we set off across the field I constructed one of those artificial questions we sometimes ask to show how much we know. I think it was something about responsories at vigils, because it was to show that though I was an Anglican I knew a thing or two. In any event, I posed my question and he stopped, looked as though he were thinking about the question, and put his hands on my shoulders and shook his head with what would I say was a slight smile and a slight sadness and he said, "Oh Franciskus, you are so very, very Anglican." And I knew I'd been found out. And it was the mixture of insight and affection that made him my *abba* on the spot.

Subsequently, I remember coming on retreats and sometimes after Compline he would say, "Franciskus, go to the kitchen and get a corkscrew and come to the Casa Abbaziale," which of course, as most of you know, was a rebuilt chicken coop. There we would have a glass of wine and talk. It was a very special time for me and a very special relationship.

When in 1968 I made my oblation, I did so in the crypt in front of a window that depicts the life of a monk, a window which, along with the others, has come to mean more and more to me over the years because the windows together depict the mystery of time. I visit the crypt every time I am here and I contemplate the windows: the days of the week, the seasons of the year, the hours of the day and the times of prayer associated with them, the life cycle of a monk and all of us who are baptized into the death and resurrection of Christ, the Paschal mystery depicted in the fourth window.

As I look at these windows and situate myself in these various dimensions of time, David's prayer comes to mind, the prayer he prayed after bringing the Ark of the Covenant to Jerusalem: "Who am I, O Lord God, that you have brought me as far as this? Yet in your sight this is still not far enough." I experience a kind of looking back, a taking stock, a realization that this is a resting place from which I go forth to a new season, a new sequence of days, seasons, hours of the day, a new dimension of living the Paschal mystery.

I also find myself again and again reflecting upon the Benedictine vow of stability: the importance of place and of staying put. And though it means something different, obviously, to the members of the community who live here, the very fact that when I come back there are familiar faces here means a tremendous amount to me. And the very fact that the place in all its dimensions is here makes it possible for me to reground myself and look backward and forward.

I realize more and more how much I can appropriate what is going on in my life by virtue of the stability of a place I know and can return to, and there, reluctantly, acknowledge that the name of the game is to be crucified with Christ so that it is no longer I who live but Christ who lives in me, and that, kicking and screaming and resisting all the way, it is possible that Christ is being formed in me, and that I am being conformed to the image of God's Son, as I hope is true of us all.

As I ponder all this, I realize being conformed to the image of Christ is a lifelong process. To use the first word in the *Rule of St. Benedict*, it is a lifelong process of *obsculta*, of listening: listening and being present, not simply to scripture or to sacrament, but listening and being present to the events of our lives because the events of our lives are, in their own way, words by which God addresses us.

Over the years three sentences have helped me to listen. The first is from Teilhard de Chardin: "By means of all created things without exception the divine assails us, penetrates us and molds us." I try to remember these words when dreary things happen or hideous e-mails are brought by breathless secretaries into my presence, asking "What are you going to do about this or that or the other thing?" I think even this is part of how I am being shaped and molded, as much as I may resent the form it takes.

The second is an observation made by an Orthodox monk when asked by a young layman what was the heart of his prayer for all of the years he had lived the monastic life. He said, "The very circumstances of your life will show you the way." And so when I want to fly away like the dove in the psalm and take my rest at some distant place, and not have to deal with where I find myself, I think: No, these very circumstances are part of God's way with me even though I may not be able to see it right now.

And the last sentence comes from a disciple of Thomas Merton, James Finley, who says, "A simple openness to the next human moment brings us into union with God in Christ."

These sentences help me to listen, to listen in the spirit in which Benedict invites us to listen.

I note here that in scripture the fundamental stance of a person or a community of faith is, of course, one of listening. The great confession of our Jewish brothers and sisters, the *Shema*, begins, "Hear O Israel the Lord is our God, the Lord alone." Every day our Jewish brothers and sisters open their ears to hear. And then the last book of the Bible, as quoted in the prologue to the *Rule*, tells us that anyone who has ears is to listen to what the Spirit is saying to the churches. And again Psalm 95, which is an integral part of vigils, invites us to harken to God's voice day by day: "If you hear his voice today do not harden your hearts." So *obsculta*, listening, is integral to our fidelity, not simply as monastics but as persons of faith baptized into the death and resurrection of Christ.

With this notion in mind of listening as a way of being shaped and formed and conformed to the image of Christ, I've reflected upon the life of St. Benedict as set out in the dialogues of St. Gregory. What we are given there is an account of listening, careful listening. The New Testament word for obey really means to listen: to listen intently; to yield yourself, surrender yourself, to what you are hearing; to harken to God's voice in whatever way it comes to us—as word or event or the circumstances in which we find ourselves. Gregory's *Life of Benedict*, written about fifty years after Benedict's death, is filled with miracles and has been discounted as real history, but I think the outline of his life may be fairly accurate.

As a young man, Benedict went to study in Rome, was horrified by Roman life and resolved to embrace the religious life. He turned his back on his studies and fled with his nurse. He later left his nurse behind and went off to a cave in Subiaco, where he was alone and concealed for three years. I think at that point he was listening to the words of the desert tradition in which people went off as solitaries to caves and isolated places and there struggled with the demons and sought to yield themselves to the will of God. As he continued his solitary life he was ministered to by a monk of a nearby monastery, who brought him bread and let it down in a basket.

At length, Gregory observes, the time came when Almighty God decided to reveal Benedict's virtuous life to others. So how does God do this? Does God send a word directly to Benedict? No, he speaks to Benedict through others. In this case (I think this is rather charming) there was a priest preparing his Easter lunch and in a vision the priest is told, "How could you prepare these delicacies for yourself while my servant is out there in the wild suffering from hunger?" So the priest is told to prepare an extra portion of Easter dinner and take it off and find Benedict. The priest arrives and says, "Today is the great feast of Easter." And Benedict replies, "It must be a great feast to have brought me this kind of a visit." And then they say grace and eat the meal. So Easter is celebrated by the sharing of a meal. I think that is a wonderful way in which the Paschal mystery is proclaimed to Benedict. There is no liturgy mentioned but just a great big meal. This is the beginning of being led out of solitude.

The next thing that happens is that some shepherds find him and think he's a wild animal. They then realize that he is not a wild animal at all, he's a servant of God. So, rather than pursuing him through the thicket, they sit down and listen and are edified by what he has to say. And this is God calling Benedict to speak a word out of the depths of his own experience of God in prayer. This is then the beginning of Benedict being turned toward the world, being taken out of his desert sense of himself into a new relationship with the human community. And we are told that many people came to visit him and changed their way of life because of his wise teaching, I wonder at this point if a certain amount of ego gratification didn't creep in here. As humble as he was it must have been in some way satisfying to have people come and say, "Oh, just a word of life, please: oh, that's so helpful."

At this point he suffers a violent temptation of the flesh, which I think knocked him down a few pegs and reminded him that he wasn't some sort of idealized desert father, but he was altogether human and had to deal with human realities, indeed even the flesh in the form of temptations. And so he rolls in the thicket and is victorious over sin and temptation and, we are told, led to a new maturity.

I think that new maturity didn't mean simply the conquest of the flesh but rather the recognition that he was a person of flesh. He made friends with the flesh. In a way, the temptation lost its power. Temptation has its power when we are terrified and do not acknowledge its presence. So often we keep secrets, even from ourselves and those secrets become a kind of power that can overwhelm us. It is by acknowledging our temptations, acknowledging our frailties, and our humanities that we then, in many instances, can be set free from the oppressive power they sometimes have over us. In any event, out of this new maturity many placed themselves under his guidance. And Gregory tells us that with the passing of this temptation Benedict's soul was like a field cleared of briars and soon yielded a rich harvest of virtues and the renown of his name increased.

So here he is in a new place, wiser, more mature, and people are coming to him. He's careful not to allow too much ego gratification to slip into his ministry. Then some monks arrive from presumably the monastery Vicovaro and say, Our monastery is an absolute mess and your reputation is well known; would you please come and be our abbot? And Benedict warns: "If I come I'm going to make some changes, because your way of life and my way of life are not congruent." And they say: "Fine; come; we need a renewal program. We need a reshaping, rethinking our ministries and our charisms, or whatever." So he becomes their abbot. They soon tire of his resolute style, his zeal, and take drastic measures. They poison a pitcher of wine on the abbot's table, but as Benedict makes the sign of the cross over it before pouring it out, the pitcher shatters and Benedict knows instinctively that it has been poisoned, and he leaves them. He says, "May Almighty God have mercy upon you," and with that he returns to the wilderness he loved.

Now I think this is probably where Benedict learns something about the limitations of humanity in community. He had gone with all this reforming zeal and been, I assume, unyielding in his application of his principles and hadn't made enough room for the human reality and the limitations of those under his care, which ultimately drove them to this drastic and extreme measure. It is my sense that out of this experience Benedict emerged in an expanded awareness of a need for proportion and prudence, of leniency. We certainly see this reflected in the *Rule*.

Along this line, I think of a story about Antony of Egypt with which some of you may be familiar. One day a visitor from afar who was on his way to visit the great Abba Antony in the desert came over a hill and saw Antony with members of his community playing with bows and arrows, obviously engaged in some kind of recreation. The visitor was horrified that they would be engaged in anything this-worldly and superficial. So he went up to Antony and said: "This is shocking that you would be out playing like this. You are meant to be men of prayer." Antony was silent—that is always the way with the desert monastics: they were silent—and he said: "Pick up the bow." The visitor picked up the bow. Antony said, "Put an arrow in it and draw it and let it go. Now quickly put another arrow in it. Now put another arrow in it. Now put another arrow in it." And the visitor finally said, "If you keep doing this, the constant tension will break the bow." And Antony replied, "And so will the human spirit break if it is never allowed to relax." Antony clearly understood the limitations of our humanity.

I think that out of his experience at Vicovaro, Benedict was led to a more temperate place in the application of his principles. In any event, at this point in the story Gregory describes Benedict as coming to live with himself: *habitare secum*. Out of this cumulative experience of being addressed through these various events and circumstances, Benedict was being matured and coming home to himself in grace and truth in a whole new way.

And so we are told that Benedict now lives in the presence of his heavenly father. I think that coming home to himself, recognizing his own tendency toward zeal, recognizing other dimensions of himself, brought him a kind of self-awareness that made him now truly wise. And I might say self-awareness is a gift of grace. It is very different from self-analysis, which is something we do to ourselves. Augustine of Hippo is very clear that self-knowledge is related to knowing God: "How can I know God without knowing myself . . . may I know you, may I know myself?"

John of the Cross says that self-knowledge is the springboard by which we rise to knowledge of God. Actually the two are the same: to know oneself in grace and truth is to know God, because one can only know oneself truly as one is embraced by God's profligate compassion and love. Benedict came home to himself and was ready for a larger ministry. So he established twelve monasteries, with twelve monks in each and in each an abbot.

The only other thing that I would add here is the wonderful encounter with his sister, Scholastica. This encounter is marvelously captured in a fresco at Subiaco in which Benedict and his sister are dining together. Benedict is looking anxious and Scholastica is looking sly and knowing. The story is as follows. Scholastica, from early childhood, was dedicated to God, was religious, and once a year she and her brother would come together to reflect on holy things and to ponder the mystery of God. On this particular visit, at the end of the day, Benedict said, "I have to go home now to the monastery," and Scholastica replied, "But brother dear, we have so much more to share about what we've experienced of God." And he said, "I really must go. I can't stay. I can't be away from the monastery overnight." So Scholastica turned her eyes heavenward, and suddenly, accompanied by lightening and thunder, a violent storm arose that made it impossible for Benedict to leave. "Sister what have you done?" he cried out and she responded, "Well, you didn't listen to me so I turned to God and this is the result." And so they talked all through the night. At this point, Gregory observes, Scholastica proved mightier, since hers was the greater love. Three days later she died and Benedict saw her soul in the form of a dove being carried to heaven. Benedict's encounter with his sister taught him something about human bonds and relaxing rules in favor of larger goods. Benedict was a learner all through his life: listening, listening, listening. The very circumstances of Benedict's life showed him the way. He listened to each encounter as the voice of invitation, the voice of God in Christ, inviting him and calling him deeply into the unfolding of God's will.

Here it is important to note that God's will, and the doing of God's will, which we often think of in terms of capitulation to divine directives, really has a very different meaning. The word "will" in Greek, *thello*, means, among other things, to feel affection for. Thus, the will of God is God's affectionate desire for us, not just "will you do this by nightfall and therefore be obedient." It's not that way at all; the will of God is God's deep desire for us. In the same manner, I have a will for my children, which is their happiness, their fulfillment, their maturity. I agonize when they seem to go in a direction I think is unwise, but I know they have to discover that on their own; and I rejoice when they do something or discover something that seems to increase them and bring them joy and greater personhood. That's what God's will is in relationship to us. God loves us deeply, and the will of God is really an expression of God's affection for us and deep desire for our full flourishing.

This richer understanding of God's will is evident in the baptismal experience of Jesus. "You are my beloved son, you are my beloved child, my chosen one in whom I rejoice." In some way God says that to each one of us and that's the heart of God's will for us.

I think that is where the *Rule of Benedict* leads us. I think that's where Benedict's own fidelity to listening led him: away from a kind of crushing asceticism into a self-welcoming sense of God's own affection that gave him a freedom that allowed him then to be a wise father, an encourager to his monks, not simply in his own day but across the years. The *Rule*, therefore, can be seen as the fruit of listening: listening to his own life, listening to the monastic and ascetic tradition that preceded him and was contemporary with him. The *Rule* is drawn from many sources, most notably the *Rule of the Master*, but it's also drawn from his own experience, his capacity, as it were, to live with himself.

As I look at the *Rule* there are several things that stand out. The first is the whole notion of conversion, *Conversatio morum*, which the Collegeville edition of the *Rule of St. Benedict* translates as fidelity to the monastic life. In an article by John E. Lawyer in *Cistercian Studies* entitled "*Conversatio* and the *Rule of St. Benedict*," the point is made that *conversatio* comes from the word *conversio*, meaning to turn around.[1] It is a passive form of the verb and it means to be turned around: to be turned around frequently. And by extension it means to have dealings with, to live with, to be shaped by. Thus it carries several levels of meaning. *Conversatio* has to do with duration, something that is ongoing and habitual; it is a process and it has to do with dynamism; it's a verb of motion, of being turned; it means something is going on all the time.

It also has a social connotation. It is usually people who knock off our rough edges, who minister the word to us, the word that converts us and turns us around. The ancient monastics of the desert used to say, "Life and death are in the hands of my brother or my sister," meaning that through one's brother, one's sister, one's fellow limb of Christ's risen body, one is sometimes accosted, one is challenged, one is supported and affirmed, one is encouraged, one is brought to a greater sense of awareness, one sees oneself more accurately through the eyes of another and in that way we are changed, which is what conversion is all about. And so *conversatio morum* is really a lifelong process.

To use a phrase from the Anglican mystic, William Law, "Conversion is the process of Christ." That is, Christ happens to us over time through others whose lives touch ours. Though this way of being informed to Christ happens with particular intensity in a monastic community, it has to do with *all* the manifestations of community in which we live as members of Christ's body. It certainly has to do with our being configured in familial patterns as well. I have been profoundly changed by my daughters, who know me better than I know myself, and can anticipate my every response before I even open my mouth. I am astonished and convicted by some of their insights.

I invite you, if you aren't familiar with it, to look at the window downstairs that depicts the life of a monk. The left-hand panel shows an overturned city surmounted by swirls of water.

The right-hand panel shows a city right-side-up with swirls of water beneath it. The swirls indicate baptism and our being turned over and upside-down and inside-out by the Paschal mystery, our being baptized into the death and resurrection of Christ. Between those two panels are a shovel, a ladder, and an altar. The shovel represents work. The ladder represents *lectio*: the rumination, the chewing over of scripture and the ancient text. The altar represents the life of prayer and sacrament. So there is work, *lectio*, prayer: body, mind, and spirit. Above we see arrows bound together, which represent community. We are Christ to one another, as Father Martin has said. Below is a crozier representing the authority of the abbot. Authority properly means the capacity to give life, and so the abbot, who represents Christ, is to be a life-giver to the community and is to speak the word of Christ in such a way that the community can hear it, receive it, and be enlivened by it. The abbot, says Matthew Kelty, himself an abbot, needs a firm hand, not a hand that crushes but a hand that protects the monk from the forces that fight against him, and his own self-destructive urges. I have found this to be true in my abbatial life as a bishop.

The whole *Rule*, therefore, is an exercise in structured listening. It describes, in Benedict's phrase, a "school for the Lord's service," in which I am still a student, with a particular emphasis on

> how to run the path of God's commandments with the heart overflowing with the inexpressible delight of love. This is a love which is poured into our hearts by the Holy Spirit, a wild, unbounded, profligate love that exceeds all that we can ask or imagine or even begin to understand because it is God's love which overwhelms all fear, all self-judgment, a love that bears all things, believes all things, hopes all things, endures all things.

Notes

1. John E. Lawyer, "*Conversatio* and the *Rule of St. Benedict*," *Cistercian Studies* 27, no. 1 (1992): 13-21.

A Voice for the Praying Church

MARY COLLINS

It is fitting to add my voice to the many voices that will be speaking words of gratitude and congratulations to our Benedictine brothers of Mt. Saviour Monastery this year, 2001. You stand among us as witnesses to God's faithfulness. In Pine City, New York, you have made visible day in and day out for half a century the wisdom of St. Benedict teaching about what it means to live well, whatever one's times and circumstances. While the world has been changing around you these past fifty years, you have shown your friends the wisdom of honoring place, honoring tradition, and honoring commitment to one another as the way to flourish from one generation to the next. Your very existence among us is a contribution of monasticism to the church and to the world, evidenced by the fact that since your early days both church and world have found their way to your home and your chapel. Congratulation! Our thanksgiving gives rise to our prayer for you: by God's mercy may you continue to flourish for uncounted years ahead.

When Prior Martin invited me to be part of this anniversary series, with the sole stipulation that I offer something from my particular interests and expertise, I determined that I should speak about liturgical praying. Praying liturgically has engaged me from my childhood and adolescence in Chicago, long before I had any words to name that interest. I consider myself blessed to have been given the opportunity as a Benedictine to study and to teach in an area for which I have always felt passion. Now, in my post-academic post as prioress of a monastic community of women, I find myself reflecting on old questions in new ways. And so my topic: A Voice for the Praying Church. Note that my claim for the Benedictines is modest: *A* Voice not *The* Voice for the Praying Church.

To pique your interest in the phenomenon of praying, let me begin with stories. I will use a biblical wisdom strategy—"three things and then a fourth." Three brief anecdotes and then a fourth that invite us to think about praying as ordinary, but also mysterious human activity. The first story is found among *The Sayings of the Desert Fathers.* Locate yourself in the fourth century Egyptian desert, where the following was recorded: A brother said to Abba Anthony, "Pray for me." The old man said to him. "I will have not mercy upon you, nor will God have any, if you yourself do not make an effort and if you do not pray to God."

The contemporary American writer Annie Dillard recounts my second story in her book-length essay on the human estate in the cosmos, named *For the Time Being.*[1] Locate yourself in eighteenth century in the company of Eastern European Hasidic Jews. Imagine, if you will, the magic and mystery of a world experienced at all times as diffused with the divine—the world of European Hasidism expressed in the stained glass and paintings of Marc Chagall. As the story goes:

> A Hasid was traveling to Miedzyboz to spend the Day of Atonement with the Baal Shem Tov in the prayer house. Nightfall caught him in an open field and forced him, to his distress, to pray alone. After the holiday, "the Baal Shem Tov received him with particular happiness and cordiality. 'Your prayer,' he said, 'lifted up all the prayers which were lying stored in that field.' "

And Dillard then adds, from Psalm 93: "The waters have lifted up their voice; / the waters have lifted up their pounding waves."

The third story brings us to our own times. Mother Irene Dabalus, the Filipino-born superior general of the Tutzing Missionary Benedictines, upon returning recently from a trip to visit her sisters in India, remarked that the Indian people have come to respect the Christian communities among them for their works of charity. But they do not think of Christians, even Benedictine missionaries, as gifted in prayer. To learn to pray even

Indian Christians will often turn to Buddhist and Hindu teachers. When I heard her remark, I remembered a rueful comment made in my presence many years ago by an American Benedictine monk: "It will be said of our times that there were many monastic vocations, but there was no room for them in our monasteries."

The fourth and final anecdote, also from the Hasidic tradition, reports the wonder of God at prayer. Rabbi Nachman of Bratslav said that God studies Torah three hours a day. The Talmud notes that God prays, and puts on phylacteries. What does God pray? "May it be my will that my mercy overcome my anger."

I savor these stories, because I have been thinking for a long time about prayer and about the praying Benedictines do. I first met Benedictines at prayer in my undergraduate college days, which began only a short time after the Mt. Saviour community was established. I remember clearly what attracted me to the Benedictine way of life lived by the women who were my college teachers. Over the course of four years we could not help but overhear them chanting the Divine Office in choir, although we never joined them. From a distance, it became evident to me that they knew something about praying, and that I could learn from them. Forty-plus years later, I am still learning. But I am now better able to understand what we Benedictines are up to, and why; and also why what we do is a gift to church and society.

The questions and some answers are summed up in those stories:

Praying is an ordinary human activity, not something for specialists. *(So Anthony.)*

Prayer rises from the whole creation. (So *the Baal Shem Tov.)*

We humans need to look for teachers of prayer. (So *Mother Irene Dabalus)*

God, too, has learned to pray wisely by spending time with Torah. *(So the Hasids)*

Our Situation: Being Human in the Cosmos

Having invited you to the Egyptian desert, to Eastern Europe, to the Philippines, let me transcend the local and particular in order to locate this reflection about Benedictines at prayer within "the big picture." For it is from within our human condition within the cosmos that we find ourselves being drawn to prayer.

In your imagination pull out the many photos you have seen of our small blue planet earth orbiting within our galaxy. Then locate that galaxy within the expanding universe of countless galaxies. If you have read astrophysicist Brian Swimme and historian of religion Thomas Berry's book *The Universe Story,* pull to consciousness their presentation of "the big picture."[2] Retrieve an awareness of the universe that astronomers and mathematicians try to conceptualize for us in models. Disney World to the contrary, it is decidedly *not* "a small world after all." When we put ourselves in "the big picture," we know that during our relatively brief lifetimes, each of us is in on a great ride within an expanding the universe. But we also know, from watching our neighbors close up, that our ride in the cosmos will be a tragic one. We will flourish and then die quickly in the cosmic scheme of things.

Again, I turn to Annie Dillard for the turn of phrase that helps us to locate ourselves as "the human kind" within the big picture. Dillard writes from the viewpoint of a modern Christian living in a scientific age. She says,

> Trafficking directly with the divine, as the manna-eating wilderness generation did, and as Jesus did, confers no immunity to death or hazard. You can live as a particle crashing about and colliding in a welter of materials with God, or you can live as a particle crashing about and colliding in a welter of materials without God. But you cannot live outside the welter of colliding materials."[3]

We know of what she speaks: AIDS, malaria, shrapnel or bullets, car crashes, explosions, floods, fires, earthquakes, clogged arteries, cancer.

It is hard to keep things in perspective, to keep looking at the cosmic picture of fatal collisions, for a whole range of reasons. Ernest Becker argued some years ago in *The Denial of Death*, that were we humans fully attentive to the conditions of our existence we would lose all human capacity to function sanely.[4] We would be unable to "get on with life." What we identify as psychological health in our time, said Becker, requires that we develop strong egos, that we become individual selves with life projects making us worthy of being remembered by posterity. To children we say, "What do you want to do when you grow up?" To adults who have been working for years we say again, "What will you do when you retire?"

But other thinkers—Dillard among them—defy the limits of "common sense," insisting that we pay attention to our condition of our human condition for the sake of true self-knowledge. Long before the modern scientific era, the psalmist wrote, and we still pray: "No matter how great, / no one sees the truth: / we die like beasts." And elsewhere in Psalm 49 we pray: "No matter how wealthy, / no matter how many tell you, / 'My, how well you have done,' / The rich all join the dead / never to see light again." Life projects carry us only so far in coming to terms with our place in the divine plan.

We know the story of the great saint Thomas Aquinas, who completed a life project on a grand scale, the kind Becker might have described as the work of a cultural hero. But upon his enlightenment concerning his place in the mystery of human being, Thomas himself devalued the ultimate significance of the great *Summa Theologica*. Ironically, it is most typically in relation to his life project that Aquinas is still remembered and celebrated.

Philosophers in every era try to assess our identity as humans. The contemporary French philosopher Julia Kristeva summarizes our paradoxical human condition in the epigram "I am mortal and I am speaking." Annie Dillard sums up our place as humans in the cosmic scheme of things. She observes, "An infant is a pucker of the earth's thin skin; so are we. We arise like budding yeasts and break off; we forget our beginnings." Another philosopher explains more abstractly how we who are "puckers of the earth that have broken off" are, nevertheless, each of us, a microcosm of the universe. In each woman and man, in each infant on planet earth is found everything that can be found in the entire cosmos, that is, both spirit and matter. Our distinction: we are that part of the universe of matter come to consciousness and responsibility.

And having come to consciousness, we humans are able to wonder intellectually at a world not of our own making that we take in through our senses. Inevitably we discover, much as we resist the discovery, that we have to die. These are the realities that evoke from us the response we call prayer. We wonder and are grateful for the gift we are and the gifts that have been given to us. But we are left dissatisfied, restless, wanting more, without knowing clearly what it is we want. Put positively, we are impelled toward self-transcendence without knowing what will satisfy, without knowing what the German theologian Karl Rahner called "the whither of our transcendence." We resist the prospect that "the I that I am" will perish, will be returned to the earth, will vanish and be seen no more. Personally, in dealing with the death of a person significant to me, I return again and again to Edna St. Vincent Millay's poem "Dirge Without Music." She opens with her theme: "I am not resigned to the shutting away of loving hearts in the hard ground." And the last stanza returns to it:

> Down, down, down into the darkness of the grave
> Gently they go, the beautiful, the tender, the kind;
> Quietly they go, the intelligent, the witty, the brave.
> I know. But I do not approve. And I am not resigned.[5]

Faced with death, we choose to live. So it is good news that the story of Jesus, the story of the death of one known as a good man, invites us to believe and to hope.

Divine Incarnation as Revelation in the Cosmos

Modern scientists have recently gotten interested in telling the story of "Spirit in the universe," the story of the dynamism of continually unfolding universe that started from nothing and gave birth to time billions of years earlier. Pre-scientific creation myths among all the world's peoples gave local accounts of how things came to be, and each generation taught the next how to respond to the mystery of existence as they understood it. Notre Dame philosopher John Dunne has proposed that all cultures are organized to respond to that disconcerting truth: humans die. As Dunne put it in *The City of the Gods*, one of his early works, each culture proposes an answer to the perennial human question: "If I must someday die, what can I do to satisfy my desire to live?"[6]

Enter the story of Christ and the church. It is the story of incarnation, the story of the breaking forth of divine spirit into human history in the person Jesus of Nazareth and the outpouring of his Holy Spirit on those who would become the church. We who believe call the person of Jesus God's definitive revelation to our humankind of our place in the cosmic mystery. We have come to believe that if we keep our eye on Jesus and open ourselves to the Holy Spirit of the risen Christ, it will be shown to us how to live well toward death in any and all times, places, and cultures. To keep our eye on Jesus and to open ourselves to the Holy Spirit of the risen Christ, so that we may live and die well, is the vocation of the Christian contemplative. It is thereby the vocation of all the baptized who have put their faith in Christ. As Abba Anthony warned the suppliant brother who had asked Anthony to pray for him: "I will have not mercy upon you, nor will God have any, if you yourself do not make an effort and if you do not pray to God"—if you are not willing to stand before mystery.

And at this point the questions of teachers of prayer are raised. How can I pray unless someone shows me? Who taught that desert brother how to pray? What was his path to the prayer of contemplation? And who has been teaching Christians in every successive generation how to pray? (Why were those seekers of God in India looking for teachers everyplace but among Christians?)

The Hasidic rabbi I referred to earlier in this essay noted that the source for God's prayer is Torah. Why should we not begin there? And what did God learn to pray for, through the faithful study of Torah? If the story is true (and what reason is there to believe the rabbis were mistaken in this reflection?) the God of Israel, who is the God of all nations, learned to pray thus: "May it be my will that my mercy overcome my anger!" Perhaps we too might pray for an abatement of anger in favor of loving kindness in our dealings with all our humankind. In summary, there are two things we can know. First, the Scriptures are a reliable teacher of prayer. And second, we pray in order to be reshaped so as to share in the heart and mind of God.

The story of monasticism from Anthony onward advances in great measure as a story of seekers of meaning for their lives, young and old, who are willing to make the effort to pray to know the heart of God, and who gather around mentors in schools of prayer. Some arrive, now as in earlier generations, knowing that "Jesus is the answer," too young or too self-confident to have a clue about the question. No matter. In Benedict's school of the Lord's service, serious seekers would learn both the question and the answer. With or without the question clearly formulated—"If I must someday die, what can I do to satisfy my desire to live"—many generations of men and women who came to Benedictine monasteries seeking God learned how to pray and so how to live.

Even before Benedict, monastic seekers of meaning for living learned the Scriptures by heart, and so learned to recognize mercy, compassion, and loving kindness through stories and songs celebrating its absence as well as its presence in human history. Living with other seekers, they also learned the practices of mercy, compassion, loving kindness—and they learned also about what happens in the absence of mercy, for they lived among human brothers and sisters who were all learning together. As monastic seekers took the biblical songs and stories to heart, they were slowly being transformed by the Spirit of Jesus. The Holy Spirit breathed in them, through those stories and songs lodged in their hearts. By Benedict's time, traditions of communal monastic prayer had formed, and it is the monastic prayer tradition we call the Divine Office or the Liturgy of the Hours, that we want to speak about now.

Official Claims Concerning the Monastic Liturgy of the Hours

Church documents of the last two centuries have repeated more than once and in a variety of settings the claim that the sole necessary work of monastic communities is prayer. The Dominican

General Timothy Radcliffe recently offered to the Congress of Abbots his observation that Benedictines as an Order in the church have "nothing in particular" to do, except pray. Unfortunately, civil authorities in modern European countries were never fully comfortable with that assertion, and in a variety of ways mandated that monastic communities needed to justify their existence by also "doing something useful"—the utility of prayer in and with Christ not being immediately evident to moderns. The women in the Bavarian community to which we Benedictine sisters at Mount St. Scholastica trace our roots made themselves useful in the nineteenth century by becoming school-teacher-monastics.

The lack of clarity about monastic identity and purpose that resulted from the pressure to be "useful" according to pre-determined cultural criteria had a cumulative negative effect on monastic communities in the nineteenth and twentieth centuries. There have been many hyphenated Benedictine monastics in the Western church. Because of the confusion, there has been a decline in the courage of hyphenated Benedictine monastics to believe that the contemplative vocation can stand on its own as a contribution to either church or society. For the most part Western Benedictines have all but succumbed to the value judgments of modern culture about what is useful. Mount Saviour's foundation story protected it somewhat from that history.

Fortunately, the call to Benedictines to do "nothing in particular" but to pursue a public vocation to contemplative prayer continues to sound. Yet the call carries with it a correlative 1confusion about the nature of contemplative prayer. Benedict's Rule provides that monastics say the prayer of the Hours. Yet aspiring contemplatives in today's Benedictine monasteries wonder. With requirements for hours of choral public prayer and for manual labor, reading, and community living, how can there be time for sitting, centering, breathing, and meditation as paths to contemplative prayer?

In the authoritative *Directory for the Celebration of the Work of God* prepared twenty-five years ago by the Congress of Benedictine Abbots, the abbots expressed no self-doubt, if they had any, about the Liturgy of the Hours as itself the Work of God, the way into the heart of God. Using the theological vocabulary of the Second Vatican Council, the *Directory* calls the praying of the Liturgy of the Hours the "proper ministry" of a monastic community. And with perhaps a nod to the die-hard utilitarians of the nineteenth and twentieth centuries, they identify the prayer of the Hours as ministry "useful for the building up of the Body of Christ."[7] Indeed, paraphrasing their assertion in contemporary economic terms, could we not say that every Benedictine liturgical gathering for the prayer of the Hours is adding value in the divine economy, the cosmic *oeconomia?*

Yet we need better to understand just what is being said about prayer as the proper ministry of Benedictines useful for the Church. How is our choral praying of the Liturgy of the Hours "a proper ministry" for the Body of Christ and the world? How is it even valuable to ourselves? We have to rule out the easy answer: whatever Benedictines are doing when we are engaged in the Work of God, the *Opus Dei*, we are not spiritual mercenaries for busy people. Abba Anthony had already warned sixteen hundred years ago that God expected each of us to make the effort ourselves. Unfortunately, the sense of being spiritual mercenaries has surfaced more than once in monastic history, as when monastic foundations were paid princely sums to pray for the salvation of their benefactors, who were themselves quite commonly engaged in counter-salvific activities.

I have been thinking again why we as twenty-first century Benedictines still commit ourselves to praying in choir as a community and call this choral praying our proper ministry. I am convinced that the ministry of the Benedictine monastery will find its expression in its willingness to be the voice of the praying church. Nevertheless, the final part of my presentation is necessarily dialogic. Any claim we might make from within the world of the Benedictine monastery must be validated by those who are the praying church within the larger human community.

Benedictine Monastics in Choir:
A Voice for the Praying Church

My first presumption is that everyone is praying, because the One we seek in our desire to live is already stirring within us. During our daily "crashing and colliding" with the materials of the universe, Spirit stirs in the whole creation. In the melee on this planet that is our home in the universe, everybody is praying, even when the words spoken sound to human ears like cursing. The psalms have succeeded in teaching us that. St. Paul goes further, assuring us that the Holy Spirit is praying at all times, with sighs too deep for words, helping us in our weakness, interceding for us when we do not know how to pray. Some of us pray aloud in choir as our distinct ministry. However, we will look at the choir only after we see the monastic choir in context.

Ride a public bus or subway during the morning rush hour. Some commuters will have bibles open in their laps; others will sit in self-contained silence, faces masked but full of interior longing or despair or delight and gratitude or perhaps seething with anger at betrayal. Human aspiration and passion, despair and happiness pervade the morning air in rush hour traffic, too. Every person we observe is linked in their interior longing or despair to unseen others in hospitals, in jails, or in the homes they have left behind.

But let's not limit ourselves as we think about the context of the Benedictine monastic choir. Paul and the psalmist and the Hasidic rabbis tell us that the striving of spirit in the world is not limited to our self-conscious humankind. The very fields are full of prayers. Wildflowers and grasses reflect back the glory of the creator. Fields with stagnant ponds and trash wait "with eager longing to be set free from bondage to decay," wait for the redemption of our humankind so that they may obtain the freedom of glory (Romans 8:18-25).

Because our humankind does not know how to pray as we ought, says Paul, the Holy Spirit helps us in our weakness. At this juncture of unknowing, the church enters in a distinctive way, and the context of the monastic choir is also the church. It is true that *spirit* is active everywhere in the universe. Yet the Holy Spirit of Jesus of Nazareth, the Risen Christ, is being continually poured out. It is this Holy Spirit of Jesus that shapes the community of the baptized, the Body of Christ on earth. The church is a community transcending every culture, yet resident in virtually all living cultures at the start of the twenty-first century. In a parallel expansion, monastic choirs have been forming for the prayer of the Hours everywhere in the southern hemisphere and in Asia.

Why this expansion of monastic choirs? Consider this possibility. The church understands itself to be a priestly people among all the peoples of the earth. But what is this priestly identity? For many generations, Catholics have equated priestly identity with ordination to church office. Yet in a much earlier era peoples and cultures have understood the role of priest as intermediary; in the words of Scripture, the priest is designated to "weep between the porch and the altar" (Joel 2:17). The priest could negotiate this connection, because it had been revealed to the priest who God was and how to approach God, voicing on behalf of others what needs to be voiced. It is within this frame that the whole church has its priestly identity, for it is to the whole church that the mystery of Christ has been disclosed, for the sake of the world. Christians, may be "puckers on the earth's thin skin," like all other humans, but we believe that we are also those "puckers" to whom the mystery of the world's salvation in Christ has been entrusted. In biblical language, we are ambassadors sent to deliver good news to the whole world, and advocates sent by Christ's Holy Spirit for the world's well-being.

It is within this frame of its priestly identity conferred at baptism that the church is impelled to "pray always." Praise and endless glory to God befit the church. But so also does lamentation with Christ for what is wounded and goes unhealed. So also is it fitting that the church plead for mercy for all humankind and intercede for forgiveness or seek consolation for what has been lost.

To underscore my point, let me ask you to return to the people praying on the subways and buses. However much they are filled with pain and longing, gratitude and delight, many if not most are short on language adequate to speak about their deepest desires and regrets. In them and in people like them all over the world, the Holy Spirit is undoubtedly praying, even as they themselves doubt that they know how to pray. Others among the commuters, having been baptized into the Body of Christ and shaped by the faith of the church, have learned how to draw the world's inarticulate longing, and their own, into focus, identifying every human experience with the life, suffering, death, and resurrection of Jesus. But the morning praying of the commuters, like the morning prayer of much of the world, is inaudible and invisible. Yet if prayer is to follow the law of Incarnation, both the inarticulate prayer of the human heart and the interior prayer of the Body of Christ stand in need of release into the world of conscious matter. The prayer of Christ needs body and voice—the body and voice of the church in human history.

Embodied human prayer has a living history. Just recently we have seen news reports of millions of Muslims embodying their desire for connection with God in their *hajj* to the Arabian desert. We have heard reports of countless Hindus bathing naked at the confluence of sacred waters at an auspicious time in their festival season. Jewish men wrapped in prayer shawls sway and chant daily at the Western Wall. Buddhists sit.

Embodied Christian prayer, too, has a living history. But Catholics and Christians generally have lost confidence in our most ancient traditions of embodied prayer, among them the Benedictine communal prayer of the Hours. Christians in modern Western cultures, including Catholic Christians, are allowing themselves to be persuaded that embodied communal prayer is antithetical to true "spirituality." True spirituality is being redefined primarily as a matter of personal interiority, so time spent praying "in" and "with" Christ for the whole of creation does not have much attraction. Ours is world where successful people are those who are able to "make it on their own."

In this context it is worthwhile to look again at the tradition of embodied prayer that Benedict offered his monastics. Monastics assemble with regularity several times daily. In assembling, they make visible locally their Christian identity as a priestly people. The priesthood they exercise in this audible song of praise, lamentation, and pleading arises from their baptism in the Spirit of Jesus. The morning and evening and midday sacrifices they raise to God are "sacrifice of praises." In solidarity with the whole of creation, the whole human community, and the whole church occupied and distracted by many other responsibilities, monastic communities are free to assemble regularly because, except for this embodied praying, monastic communities have "nothing in particular" to do.

Like God, if Rabbi Nachman of Braslav had it right, Benedictine monastic communities at prayer stay close to the sacred text, so that they come to understand more and more clearly themselves what it is that God wants and how they should be approaching God on behalf of the world. Staying close to the biblical Word of God, the shared heart of the monastic community is worked over daily by the Holy Spirit, and individual monastics are invited to put on the mind of Christ themselves, but not without difficulty. As St. Augustine knew, our praying the psalms does not have as its purpose the edification of God, but rather the purpose of directing our human desire toward what God desires. He and many other early monastic teachers of prayer, including Benedict, recognized that praying the daily Office and living from the biblical words being voiced, being heard, and shaping one's heart was a sure path to the formation of the contemplative Christian.

The "Usefulness" of Benedictine Monasteries in the Ministry of Prayer

People everywhere are seeking spiritual formation and spiritual direction. Researchers and general cultural observers agree that our nation is currently caught up in a quest for "spirituality" and a hunger for things "traditional." This is specially the case for young people and young adults who experience themselves as ungrounded in the cosmic colliding that is human existence. They are searching everywhere for roots, for meaning, and for traditions. They often search alone. The parish church and the local congregations fail to touch many of them. They suspect there is something more, and they are on the lookout for guides, mentors, gurus—people who seem to "know." Books, tapes, short workshops available on the open market promise them sure and relatively painless paths to spiritual enlightenment. In their search for spiritual enlightenment they are vulnerable to charlatans and self-promoters, to spiritual "fads" and to religious romanticism, as we all were in our youth.

The Benedictine community at daily prayer, gathered several times daily, voices the traditional prayer of the church, the prayer of the Body of Christ. In our public praying we offer seekers alternative understandings of spiritual discipline and of the prayer of Christ. So, if the twenty-first century Benedictine community gathered for the Prayer of the Hours is to be a community ministering especially while it is praying, such a community in the United States will have to exercise generous welcome and attentive hospitality to those who wish to join them for prayer. To welcome others is to invite them into the heart of God and the mystery of the divine plan.

Monastic communities at prayer have the freedom to be visibly ecumenical. At the Prayer of the Hours, there is no need to warn Christians of other communions of our separation nor of formal boundaries we must honor, as is the case with our current Catholic eucharistic discipline. The Hours are voiced not only *for* but *with* whatever part of the disunited and divided praying church wishes to join us. This is a prayer that overcomes and transcends the boundaries and barriers which separate Christians.

This is also a communal prayer that affirms the identity of all the baptized as one priestly people. In an era when ecclesiastical rank is known to rankle, and tensions grow up between the ordained and the "merely baptized," the Prayer of the Hours shows the church to itself as a priestly people joined in the prayer of Christ. All together sound the laments of our humankind; all together sing praise; all together give thanks; all together ask for deliverance, forgiveness, and divine mercy. Hospitality extended to the whole church at the prayer of the Hours can be both evangelical and healing for Christians struggling with their Catholic identity.

Just as ecclesial, Christian, and Catholic identity can be discovered in the praying of the Liturgy of the Hours, so also does this prayer affirm and deepen the monastic identity of those who have publicly promised Benedictine monastic *conversatio*. Let me make two observations here. First, the Hours are communal, and the gathering by the community hour after hour, day by day, year in and year out, is itself a community-forming practice. Community-forming practices in a Benedictine monastery are ascetic disciplines, opportunities for mutual forebearance, for welcoming the mysterious Other, summoning the individual monastic beyond self-satisfaction, deeper into the Paschal Mystery, where new life opens up through dying to self.

Second, the chanting of the biblical word is an induction into the heart of God, where mercy and compassion prevail over anger. Chanting the biblical words faithfully, Benedictines privileged to voice the prayer of the whole Church are invited to understand that the creator of the universe knows and accepts our humankind better than we know and accept ourselves. To come to know this mystery and to believe it is to be a contemplative Christian, a mystic. Gregory the Great tells us that Benedict at the end of his life saw the whole world suffused in light. Gregory tells us that Scholastica knew that the heart of God was loving-kindness and that even the storm and the rain clouds conspired to let love prevail. Thomas Merton, at least for a moment, saw the people of Louisville bathed in radiance.

Benedictine communities within which the mystery of God is heartfelt because it is being heard and received, with however great difficulty or ease, will be places that attract others. Such communities are attractive because they "know something." However inarticulate monastics are, people seeking "spirituality" will find monastic communities. In the past visitors were often satisfied to have placed themselves, however, uncomprehendingly, in the monastic presence. At present, in our new cultural circumstances I doubt if that is any longer enough. Seekers want and need more from us.

The Catholic people's identity, ordained and lay, needs to be suffused with the message of divine compassion and loving-kindness. The ministry of prayer already affirmed—that we Benedictines faithfully give voice to the praying church—may be evolving, not by our design but in response to the church's great need in our time and place. What would it mean for Benedictine monasteries, now located on every continent on the globe, intentionally to commit ourselves to become, in whatever formal or informal ways are appropriate, local schools for prayer? Our world needs places where mercy and compassion and loving-kindness for the world's suffering are able to be linked directly to the prayer of Christ and the mystery of the divine design. The people of central New York are already blessed that Mount Saviour Monastery ventured onto this path fifty years ago. *Ad multos annos.*

Notes

1. Annie Dillard, *For the Time Being* (New York: Knopf, 1999).

2. Brian Swimme and Thomas Berry, *The Universe Story* (San Francisco: Harper, 1994).

3. Dillard, *For the Time Being*, 118.

4. Ernest Becker, *The Denial of Death* (New York: Free Press, 1973).

5. Edna St. Vincent Millay, "Dirge Without Music," in *The Buck in the Snow and Other Poems* (New York: Harper and Row, 1950).

6. John Dunne, *The City of the Gods* (Notre Dame: University of Notre Dame Press, 1978).

7. *Directory for the Celebration of the Work of God* (Congress of Benedictine Abbots, 1976), #14.

The Contribution of Monastic Life to the Church and World

Jeremy Driscoll

From *The Dialogues* of St. Gregory we know the little there is to know of the life of St. Benedict. St. Gregory tells us how, shortly before his death, St. Benedict had a magnificent vision in which he contemplated the whole world as contained within a single ray of light. Think about this image. St. Benedict was grasping the meaning of the whole world within something larger than itself. He was understanding it within the light of Christ, and his whole monastic life had been a preparation for this contemplative grasp. Let this serve as an image of what I wish to focus on; namely, the vision of Church and world that monastic life makes possible. It is in a particular kind of vision of the Church and the world that monastic life can make its particular contribution.

I will return to this image shortly. But first let me indicate how I wish to talk about the theme assigned to me, the contribution of monastic life to Church and world. On the occasion of the anniversary of a founding of a monastery, the tendency is to speak of history, and I will do so: What has the contribution been? But I would like to do so especially with a view toward the present and future: What can the contribution be now and in the future?

The monk is a "type" (or archetype) in the technical sense of the term. All societies, be they ecclesial or ssecular, have their types: the tiller of the soil, the hunter, the warrior, politician, poet, sage, king, queen, monk, and so on. To speak about the monastic contribution to Church and world, I want to begin here and not simply with a Benedictine focus. The Benedictine special something—whatever it is—is best understood when it avoids being too focused on itself. So, the first question becomes what has been and what can be the contribution to the Church and world of the monk as a type?

We in the West say "monastic" and are inclined to think immediately of St. Benedict, but we need to be aware that he comes as a sort of culmination and turning point in a movement that was several centuries in development before him. One of the areas of primitive pre-Benedictine monasticism that is particularly useful to examine is its relationship to ancient philosophy. The monastic movement took much from the spirit of Greek philosophy, just as the whole Christian Church did. It could do so because this philosophy was profoundly religious and spiritual. It was a being in love with wisdom, a conversion toward wisdom, to which one dedicated one's whole life. Pierre Hadot describes ancient philosophy as "spiritual exercises," exercises whose purpose was to teach those who love wisdom how to live, how to dialogue, how to die, and how to read.[1] Philosophy for the ancients was not a body of abstract ideas to toy with. It was mainly about a way of living that enabled one to think right thoughts, thus to arrive at truth.

The fourth-century Christian monasticism of the Egyptian, Palestinian, and Syrian deserts was an asceticism that replaced martyrdom at the time of the imperial Church in the first half of the fourth century. But through the Cappadocians (Basil and the two Gregorys) and then Evagrius Ponticus, the asceticism of the desert came to be understood as moving within a trajectory similar to and directly related to Greek philosophy conceived as a spiritual exercise. Thus Christian asceticism receives a refined focus: asceticism as a way of living that enabled the Christian to think right thoughts, thus to arrive at the truth that is in Christ Jesus. The Christian scriptures became for the desert monks the main text around how to live, how to dialogue, how to die, and how to read. Thus, the desert monks, who dedicated their entire lives to this "philosophical" search, bequeathed to the whole Church a tremendous patrimony of slowly acquired spiritual wisdom based on the scriptures, but much refined by the precision of thought that Greek philosophy promoted. The doctrine of the Holy Trinity, as articulated in the debates surrounding the Council of Constantinople in 381, also owes much to the Greek philosophical tradition. And so toward the end of the fourth century, monasticism became an actual spiritual workshop where one learned how to live, how to dialogue, how to die, and how to read the mystery of the Holy Trinity in all of life.

It is within this most swift and powerful of rivers that the sixth-century monasticism of St. Benedict is to be located. In a way that is most admirable for its practicality, St. Benedict arranged a way of life suited to people of his time, less immediately sensitive to the Greek philosophical patrimony, that enabled them to continue this search for divine wisdom. We are not here today to speak of the specific doctrines that are found in the Holy Rule. Specific doctrines aside, the contribution of the Holy Rule to Church and world is felt already in the whole way of life that Benedict organizes. He arranges the monk's day in such a way that it is saturated by the sacred scriptures, in the divine office, in *lectio divina*, in the pervasive silence that is designed to let his world sink down ever more deeply. Benedict's monks were also learning (1) how to live, (2) how to dialogue, (3) how to die, and (4) how to read the mystery of the Holy Trinity in all of life.

Let us return to St. Benedict's vision. Think again about this image of a world contained in a ray of light. In effect it shows us a wonderful paradox of the Christian life. By virtue of the Christian's participation in the resurrection of Christ, the heart of the Christian becomes in a very real sense larger than the world. Before Christ and the divine life that he brought to earth, we can say, rather naturally, that the world is a macrocosm within which each human being is its microcosm. The world is big, and each of us is small, each a small world. But in Christ, nothing less than the very being of God is placed in the human heart. In this way, then, each believing person becomes the macrocosm and the world its microcosm. This is what is signified in the vision of Benedict. The whole world can be seen in a single glance in Christ. It is beautiful and stunning and something to be loved, but in Christ my heart becomes bigger than the world and contains it. This is the monk-as-type in that technical sense in which I wish to use the term. The monk is meant to behold the world in a single contemplative glance and to contain it within something larger, something larger that paradoxically lies within. As C.S. Lewis reveals in his children's story, *The Nannia Chronicles*, the inside is bigger than the outside. And although a type must live the reality of his calling, the type embodies a truth that is valid for the whole society. Others too can learn the monk's vision. When this happens, it can be called the monastic contribution.

It is in this perspective that we can understand the contribution of the monastic practice of *lectio divina*, the prayerful reading of Scripture. Reading the scriptures is, among other things, about reading the world, seeking to uncover its deepest meaning. And one discovers through the sacred texts that the heart of the reader is made ever larger, such that it in fact becomes larger than the whole world; for the heart of the reader becomes the temple of Trinitarian love. *Lectio divina* was conducted in the monastic centuries with the Canticle of Canticles as the centerpiece of the whole effort. Every word was referred to Christ as to a bride-groom and understood to be potentially "a kiss from his mouth" (Canticles 1:2), and every desire to understand the text was nothing less than the bride, the soul, seeking her lover wherever he roams. Thus, what makes the heart large enough to contain the whole world is love itself, my love for Christ and my astonish-ment, like the bride of the Canticle, that he finds me beautiful. It is to this that we can refer the words at the end of the Prologue of St. Benedict's Rule: "As we advance in this way of life and in faith our hearts enlarge and we run the path of the command-ments of God filled with the inexpressible sweetness of love" (Prologue 49).

The monk as a type is a very broad category and history shows us many versions. But this is not because the category is vague. This is individual freedom that the search for God both demands and brings about. In fact, what we admire in the great monastics from the past or in contemporary examples is the attainment of inner freedom that their lives demonstrate. The real monk is the one who is free to do whatever God calls him to do, and no institutional forms can ultimately pin this grace down. More often than not, the monk will live in a monastery and take up the obligations of community life and work, but there are monks who abandon even this and live entirely alone or wander from place to place. In some rare cases the freedom is so radical that Church and society no longer can officially identify the monk as such. Anonymous, as it were, this absolutely free monk lives an intimate rapport with God in complete secrecy. Or in a different direction, a monk may take up the ministries of preaching, teaching, or even social work. But what identifies the monk in this and distinguishes him from others who practice the same profession is the witness to a radical freedom that corresponds to divine transcendence. The monk must somehow be seen to belong to God alone.

Nonetheless, we should not speak for long of the monk as type without coming to grips with the distinguishing characteristics of the Christian monk. What I have said about the monk thus far could apply for the most part to the monastic phenomenon of many religions. Among other things, this explains the tremendous potential for interreligious dialogue in monastic settings. Yet leaving that fruitful possibility aside for the moment—and preparing a solid foundation for it—I would like to indicate the specifically Christian features of the monastic phenomenon.

Facing the question theologically, as opposed to examining the practical use of these texts, the heart of the matter can be expressed thus: the Christian monk has a special calling to witness to the resurrection of Jesus Christ from the dead. Of course, every Christian is called to be a witness to this, but each in a particular way. The monk is called to this witnessing as one summoned beyond all signs, as one whose entire way of life offers clues to a reality that is infinitely transcendent, as one who wrestles at ever greater depth with the terrifying and joyful paradox that the risen Lord is met precisely in the experience of his absence to all merely carnal modes of detecting him. As St. Paul once exclaimed, "If once we knew Christ according to the flesh, we no longer know him in this way" (2 Corinthians 5:16).

But let me try to be more concrete in speaking of what is not concrete in any ordinary sense of the term. I would propose to you the image of Mary Magdalene at the tomb on Easter morning as one image that can give us some sense of this particular monastic witness. (It should be obvious here, from the very example I take, which is not exclusively monastic, that if I am speaking of the monk as a Christian type, then what I say applies to all Christians; and the monk exists simply to provide the service of being a particularly clear instance of it.)

Part of the raw material that slowly and painfully is stitched together to form the type of the Christian monk is the struggle through a lifetime to face, however it may come, the paradox of the presence of Christ precisely through his absence. This presence-in-absence continually deepens as the years pass. It is like a grid pulled down through the particular life story of each monk in his particular monastery, with its own unfolding history through the days and years; and this grid slowly molds the type of one whose whole being begins to bear the shape of presence-in-absence. In this precise way the monk becomes witness to the Resurrection. But if it is a paradox that is continually deepened, then this means that the monk is made to live an ever greater sense of absence of his Lord; and precisely in this way does he come to know the unexpected joy and wonder of his presence.

The gospel scene of the Magdalene at the tomb helps us to gauge the theological significance of this archetypal struggle. The risen Lord, who is not in the tomb, will nonetheless manifest himself there. It is a manifestation that unfolds in stages. First two angels appear there in dazzling robes. Their very presence is an eloquent, though wordless, discourse. They make visible the glory of his absence, a glory that issues indirectly from the tomb itself precisely because it is empty. In the angels the one who has disappeared from there is present in an inexpressible way. Holy is the place of his absence! Holy, the monastery; holy, the monk's heart—the place of his absence! "He is not here!"

In the next stage of manifestation the Lord himself appears, but the vision is veiled, and he is unrecognized. Yet it is he, the glorious Lord but mistaken for a gardener. But therein lies a lesson for the monk, and so for the Church, in every age, repeated in other resurrection appearances and anticipated in the teaching of Jesus: as risen Lord he is present and goes along with us in our ordinary time, making his way along the road to Emmaus (Luke 24:13-35), being hungry and naked or fed and clothed in the least of his brothers and sisters (Matthew 25:31-46), or standing there as a gardener (John 20:15).

The final stage is unveiled vision. He is recognized then as the Good Shepherd, who knows his sheep and calls them each by name (John 10:3), he calls her name, "Mary" (John 20:16). In that instant something deep within her shifts utterly. Weeping is exchanged for sheer joy, and the tomb becomes the place of the manifestation of the Living One. All this is expressed in his name pronounced by one who loves him: "Jesus! Rabboni!" (John 20:16). Here again we have an archetypal description of a monk: one who unexpectedly hears his name uttered by Christ in the depths of his being, one who utters in response the name of Jesus from those same depths.

Nonetheless, this unveiled vision takes place mysteriously in what is also an act of withdrawal—"Do not cling to me" (John 20:17)—and in the assignment of a mission: "Go and tell my brothers" (John 20:17). The freedom of the Resurrection tolerates no confining, no assurances based on what can be isolated in a particular and only here and now, a visible something, a tangible something. For he is ascending to his Father (John 20:17), that is, he is filling the universe in all its parts (Ephesians 4:10). He is Lord everywhere and in every time, saying "do not cling to me, then, in this one place and in this one time." Rather, the Lord turns Mary's attention from his "localized self" to his brothers in a mission, just as he vanished immediately upon recognition by the two disciples on the road to Emmaus so that they too could hurry out and announce the message (Luke 24:31-33). The angels who ask, "Why are you looking for him here in a tomb?" will also ask on the day of Ascension, "Why are you looking up to the sky?" (Compare Luke 24:5 with Acts 1:11). Everywhere the Lord and his angel messengers are urging us toward the mission of announcing that he is risen. This is the "going to Galilee" of which the risen Lord speaks in another Gospel, that is, the going everywhere, away from this tomb. "Tell them to go to Galilee, and they will see me there" (Matthew 28:10). Not in a tomb, not in the heavens, not clinging to me here, but in the mission of announcing this Good News.

According to an ancient sensitivity cultivated in monastic life, in the monastery there are angels present, who without words help the monks to take the measure of their place; namely, that "he is not here," that is, he is not in this world of death, not here as a corpse that we might view, not here as someone to whom we may cling. And yet he is here in his own sovereign way, here but unrecognized in the gardener sitting next to you. Not clinging to him, not placing one's fingers in his hands and side as did Thomas, but seeing only the empty tomb that is this whole carnal world, monks are meant to put their trust in the Lord's words: "Blessed are those who do not see and yet believe" (John 20:29).

All that I have suggested here about what the Magdalene shows us of monastic life can be played again, briefly, in the key of St. Benedict's vision. The monk is one who slowly learns that there is nothing in this world to which he may cling, that virtually every thing, every person, every experience will continue to whisper to him what the angels said to Mary: "He is not here. Why do you search for the Living One among the dead?" (Luke 24:5). Obedient to this experience, even while being deeply disappointed and sometimes pushed to a desperate and tearful searching, the monk may suddenly, in some completely unaccountable way, meet the Lord for whom he searches. Yet wherever the monk meets him, there is simultaneously the Lord's act of withdrawal. Thus, though he is surely met in some particular here and now, he may not be clung to there. As he withdraws, he draws the monk along with him, such that eventually the monk looks back at the whole world and sees it all in the light of the one who is ever drawing him beyond it. Every bit of the world at that point becomes precious to the monk, not as the goal of his ultimate search but as the treasured particular something in terms of which he has come to know—and without which terms he would never know—that "He is not here, he is risen." The whole world is contained within this larger light, light that is nothing less than "Christ filling the universe in all its parts" (Ephesians 4:10).

If there is a monastic contribution to the Church and world, it is to put the world in its perspective, to put it in its place, as it were; to point to the beyond-this-world, and yet to do so in such a way that every particular piece of the transcended world is suffused with the resurrection light that gives it its meaning and preserves it from death and disappearance. What ultimately preserves the world—that is, saves it—is precisely the fact that every piece of it shall have once been the particular place in terms of which the final message can be continually uttered: "He is not here, he is risen."

Well and good. Even beautiful, perhaps. Yet possibly I have gotten too quickly beyond this world to provide something tangible and fruitful with my reflections. So, we return to the here and now of the monastery and monastic practices. I have tried to come quickly and honestly to the real heart of the monastic matter, to its inner essence. With what I have suggested we can revisit some familiar monastic practices and experiences.

Let us begin with what guests experience at a monastery, for here we must surely be close to at least the raw material of whatever may be the monastic contribution to what lies beyond it. Guests are drawn to monasteries because, to put it in terms of the title assigned to these reflections, there is something that the monastery can contribute to them, be they believers (Church) or not (world). But what is it? What draws them? What do they receive? Whatever it is, I think that, in the reflections I have developed thus far, I have already indicated the secret of how it comes about. But let us try now to be a little more empirical, less theoretical.

Guests through the centuries have often told monastics what they experience at their monasteries. Despite the difference of epochs and places and styles and sizes of monasteries, this testimony tends to fall into the same pattern, suggesting that there really is a particular "something" that monasteries commonly impart. There is a monastic smell to things, generally (and thankfully) a sweet odor that is probably best described with the simple expression "monastic peace." There is a silence and calm about the place that has been drawn out by the long years of steady, stable practice of monastic life in this particular here. The tradition of monastic architecture contributes much to this. A monastery is often a model of what is meant to be the peaceful interchange and loving dialogue between human beings and the little piece of the earth they are privileged to inhabit, a place they share with other living creatures, and with the plants, the rocks, and the trees. The weather and the seasons and the years pass over them all; they survive it together, enjoy it together.

Participating in or assisting at the chanting of the Hours of the Divine Office holds a special attraction for guests. Perhaps especially those offices of the very early morning or of the depths of the night give to guests a sense that they have discovered a singular secret whose power quietly pulses beneath the surface of the world's activities and perhaps also somehow holds it in place.

These are just two examples—the sense of place and the chanting of the Hours—that can indicate the kind of dialogue in which a monastic contribution might be offered to Church and world. There are ancient wisdoms carried in these and other practices which, if attended to, can be useful and challenging to others—individuals and society at large. Yet even here the dominating paradox of presence and absence is not far from any explanation or understanding of how and why this all works. For example, it can often be the case that guests may experience a tremendous, tangible grace—monastic peace, if you will—in assisting at the chants, while that very day and those very hours of chanting may have been particularly trying for the monastic community itself. What seems an absence for the monks is tangible presence for the guests. You may be sure that if a monastery has been in a place for a long time and has faithfully persevered in the round of prayers that its rule of life requires, then this paradox has repeated itself many times. You may be sure also of finding this same paradox lived also by any individual monk who has persevered longer than the novitiate.

This paradox extends as well to the example of the monastery as a place. Wherever a monastery imparts a tangible sense of the divine presence precisely in terms of the beautiful interchange between human beings and all the natural features of this particular site, then once again, behind it lies the asceticism of the work and struggle that brought it about, hours and years in which many who contributed felt very little of what others feel now.

I am not at all suggesting that monks are always suffering and guests are always enjoying the fruit. My point goes past such an obviously mistaken simplification. I am trying to understand where the "fruit" comes from, fruit that I am calling the monastic contribution. My suggestion is that if there has been fruit and if there is to be fruit in the future, we must understand where it comes from and what produces it. Fruit comes from hoeing, pruning, watering, waiting, wondering, and worrying if something might not destroy it as it is coming to maturity. Fruit comes from its absence, slowly emerging from it with unaccountable beauty.

In these reflections I am slowly circling around and articulating good old-fashioned monastic doctrines that Benedict's monasticism provides a way of actually living out. These doctrines form a pattern; they give a concrete shape to the monastic life. It is what Benedict calls in the Prologue of the *Holy Rule*, "sharing by patience in the sufferings of Christ in the monastery until death so that one may share also in the glory of his kingdom" (50). Such doctrines are the very center of the content of sacred scripture, whose center is Christ, whose center in his Paschal Mystery. It is no accident then that monastic life has been sustained through the centuries by the practice of *lectio divina*, the prayerful reading of the Scripture. St. Benedict's daily schedule provides for several hours of each monk's day to be passed in this slow, meditative pondering of the sacred text, not to mention the several hours more in choir, where the chants are primarily composed also of scriptural texts. It is in this sustained encounter with the Word of God that the monk is slowly led by the Spirit ever more deeply into the paradox of presence-in-absence. By the Scripture he is instructed in all its ins and outs.

The Dialogues of St. Gregory provide us with yet another image of St. Benedict that can serve as a representative summary of how the monastic practice of reading might also be a contribution to Church and world. The scene that Gregory describes begins with St. Benedict seated quietly at the door of his monastery, absorbed in reading (II, 31).[2] Suddenly, crashing unexpectedly into the peace of the scene, there comes riding up on a horse a rough-mannered and haughty barbarian, shoving before him a poor peasant, who is bound with ropes. The peasant owes the barbarian money and has claimed that his goods are deposited in the safekeeping of Benedict's monastery. Without any introduction or any attempt at graciousness, the barbarian shouts at Benedict, "Get up! Get up! No tricks, just get me this scum's money, which he says you have."[3]

What follows is important for our understanding of the power of the practice of *lectio*. I would call it an quintessential monastic moment. It is, if you will, the monastic contribution to the world, here represented in one of its unhappier aspects by the barbarian. We are told that, in response to the barbarian's rude and abrupt command, St. Benedict calmly raised his eyes from his reading and looked for a moment at the barbarian. Slowly his gaze turned toward the poor peasant, noting how cruelly he was bound. Here too the task of monastic reading is represented: the monk, looking up from Scripture, fixes his gaze on the suffering of the world. In that moment in which Benedict's eyes fall on the suffering man—let us call it the moment in which the light of Scripture penetrates the darkness of human suffering and injustice—a tremendous wonder is worked. The knots in the ropes that bound the man suddenly unravel, and he stands there completely free. He, of course, was not displeased; and the barbarian was terribly impressed. This latter threw himself at St. Benedict's feet, asking for his prayers. Benedict effortlessly returned to his reading, ordering several of the monks to prepare some refreshment for the barbarian. As he was about to depart, Benedict simply took the occasion to tell him not to treat others so cruelly. So, how to state the monastic contribution? In the midst of the massive inhumanity we direct toward one another, to stay calmly anchored in the Word of God and to let its power set us free.

If we speak at too much length of the great example of the monastic saints or of the features of the monk as type, we may tend perhaps to say only good things about monks, which, of course, is unrealistic. No real monk considers himself a saint or a worthy representation of the type. The monk's disappointment and dissatisfaction with himself is an essential dimension of the monastic experience, and here too there are even possibilities for a contribution to others.

One of the surprises for the new monk is that as he makes progress in the life, he will be made to learn to regard himself more and more as a sinner. This becomes a kind of crisis; for after all, one has come to the monastery to leave sin behind and to advance toward the good. Yet after a while, one wonders if this noble project is really possible. In fact, it is not possible if it is conceived too simplistically. The life relentlessly forces the monk to abandon simplistic conceptions. A story from the desert fathers illustrates in a representative way how this necessary crisis is provoked. A brother asked Abba Poemen, "How can I think of myself as less good than a murderer?" It is a fair question, I think. Murder is an appalling sin. Can a well-behaved monk sincerely regard himself as worse than a murderer? Listen to Abba Poemen's unsettling response: "When a monk sees a man committing a murder, he should say, 'He has only committed this one sin, but I commit murder every day.' "[4]

A tremendous amount of monastic wisdom is packed into Poemen's pithy response. At first glance, it may seem that Poemen is simply requiring only a sort of pious play-acting. Murder every day? Who commits murder every day? The desert fathers knew that their unexpected formulations would rattle their disciples; they were designed precisely to do so. They also hid within their teachings scriptural treasures that could be discovered by the disciple who pondered the abba's word and tried to take it seriously. Working with Poemen's words here, the meditating mind sooner or later finds its way to the words of Jesus in the Sermon on the Mount. Jesus has recalled the commandment, "Thou shall not kill; whoever kills will be liable to judgment"; and then he immediately adds his "but." "But I say to you, whoever is angry with his brother will be liable to judgment . . . and whoever says, 'You fool' to him will be liable to fiery Gehenna" (Matthew 5:27-28). Against this new standard of obeying the commandments that Jesus establishes, no monk measures up very well; for sin is in the human heart and not merely in an exterior disobedience to commandments. The monk's heart is made of the same stuff as every other human heart. For that reason he may never regard himself, as the publican did, as "not like the rest of humanity" (Luke 18:11). By the same token, the struggle against sin that is waged in the monk's heart can take on archetypal significance.

In fact, the monk is called to a limitless empathy with the human condition. He must see himself as standing in complete solidarity with his wayward race, and this not by some act of condescension but simply in virtue of the truth of things. The mistake that the questioner of Poemen made was to have posed a comparison between himself and others. What the monk comes to realize with a sort of terrifying clarity, in his prayer and in his whole living of the monastic life, is that one cannot stand before God and point to others saying, "They are worse than me." It may well be true, but it is never relevant. Standing before God, every person is unique; each has received gifts, talents, a time, a place, a country, a culture. But there is something terribly wrong in the world; we are terribly affected by sin. And when anyone stands under the light of God's truth, that one can only cry out, as did the tax collector, "O God, be merciful to me a sinner" (Luke 18:13).

No one comes naturally to the uttering of such a prayer. Increasing the depth of conviction of oneself as a sinner is a real struggle. If I call the monk's struggle with this "archetypal," then I mean to imply that his vocation requires more than other vocations that he explore this experience to its very depths. This is not an exploration that he undertakes for himself alone, even if by its very nature it is concentrated there. The monk who pursues this way, conscious of his solidarity with the whole human condition, is able in some representative way to repent also for those who feel no need to repent; likewise he is able to receive forgiveness also for those who have not even asked for pardon. But there is more. For joy unexpectedly emerges from the darkest and most sinful depths of the human condition. Why? How? Precisely because this is the place to which the Lord himself descended when he emptied himself of glory and became sin for our sake (cf. Philippians 2:6; 2 Corinthians 5:21), and it is precisely from this place to where in death he stands in complete solidarity with us in our waywardness, that the mystery of his resurrection begins to emerge. Oh, the sheer gratuity of this joy! Infinite, divine love flooding suddenly into the heart that sees with deadly accuracy all its capacity for sin. Each monk's heart becomes the place of that dramatic combat of which the Easter sequence sings: *Mors et vita duello conflixere mirando, dux vitae mortuus regnat vivus.* "Death and life are gripped in a tremendous duel; the leader of life, having died, reigns alive."

We have come full circle. Presence and absence. The monk sees himself as sinner and so suffers the absence of God, and precisely there is God's presence unexpectedly known. But this is no private or solitary experience, even if it is intensely personal. For the monk is gazing on the whole world in the midst of his combat, and he suddenly sees the whole world caught up in a single ray of light. That light is nothing less than Christ himself. That light is the same light that unaccountably began to shine in his own darkness. It is the joy for which he never could have hoped when he was in sorrow. The light that embraces the monk is embracing the whole world. This is all grace. The monk has contributed nothing to bringing it about. But if somehow monastic life could keep the Church and world focused on this hope, then that perhaps would be a contribution.

For fifty years monastic life has been lived on this piece of the plane, Mount Saviour. We honor the monks of this community, living and dead; and we thank them for their contribution. In the secret story of all their struggles, the Church and the whole world is caught up in the light of its Savior.

Notes

1. Pierre Hadot, *Exercises spirituels et philosophie antique*, 2nd edition (Paris, 1987), 14-74.

2. St. Gregory, *Dialogues*, II, 31. In what follows, I am inspired in part by Benoit Standaert, *Les trois colonnes du monde, carnet de route pourle pelerin du XXI siecle* (Paris: Desclee, 1987).

3. I am paraphrasing loosely, but I think thus to have captured the feel of the text.

4. *Poemen 97*. See Kathleen Norris, *Amazing Grace: A Vocabulary of Faith* (New York: Riverhead Books, 1998).

Philosophy to Poetry:
Faith as a Way of Knowing in John of the Cross and Edith Stein

DAVID B. BURRELL

We are gifted with teachers and guides, companions and friends, present to us whether currently living or not, who shape our lives by giving us the courage to live and to love. As a matrix of such relationships, Mount Saviour Monastery offers a microcosm of living into and out of the perennial source of nourishment that we call "tradition." In this often cacophonous reach for symphony many voices contend, each bringing something needed, though not always appreciated. The letters of Edith Stein, as daughter, student, companion, teacher, and then as Teresa Benedicta of the Cross, testify to a person replete with friends, nourished by relationships which she herself cultivated. Responding to the initial invitation of another Teresa to collaborate in the reform of Carmel, John of the Cross devoted the bulk of his life as a religious to that work, carrying out assigned duties in the order despite acute and recriminatory opposition, yet never allowed any of it to displace his vocation as a spiritual guide. Indeed, his two most lyrical works, *The Spiritual Canticle* and *The Living Flame of Love*, were composed at the behest of friends who had come to accompany him in the spirit: Ana de Jesús and Doña Ana de Peñalosa.

The plot thickens as Edith Stein, also called forth on the journey which led her to become Sister Teresa Benedicta by her encounter with Teresa de Avila, devotes what were to be the final months of her life attempting "to understand John of the Cross in his life and works, considering him from a point of view that enables us to envisage this unity." Occasioned by the upcoming fourth centenary of the saint, this philosopher would seize that opportunity to "penetrate to this unity" of John's life and works, incorporating "an interpretation, offering what she believes a lifetime of effort to have taught her about the lows of intellectual and spiritual. being and life." So she will not hesitate to expound "her theories on spirit, faith, and contemplation," specifying that "what [she says] on ego, freedom, and person is not derived from the writings of our holy Father John . . . for only modern philosophy has set itself the task of working out a philosophy of the person such as is suggested in the passages just mentioned."[1] So this relationship of master-disciple, sustained by the family of Carmel extended over space and time, allows the apprentice to exercise her own experience coupled to philosophical developments achieved in the intervening four centuries. So the relationship between these two—a poet with an exquisite grasp of matters in philosophical theology, and a vigorous philosopher brought through her interior life to a refined sensibility for the poetics of love—can epitomize our thesis about the fruitfulness of lives lived in so rich a community of prayer and inquiry.

In attempting an appreciation of the homage of this philosophical spirit to her poetic guide and predecessor in Carmel, I shall utilize a work completed a few years before, *Finite and Eternal Being: Attempting an Ascent to the Meaning of Being*, which followed her self-imposed task of appropriating the thought of Thomas Aquinas by translating his *Disputed Questions on Truth*. The later synthetic work on the metaphysics of Aquinas owes an express gratitude to Erich Przywara's *Analogia Entis*, a work which presaged the fruitful efforts of Louis Geiger and Cornelius Fabro to call attention to the centrality of *participation* in the metaphysics of Thomas Aquinas. What is remarkable about Edith Stein's inquiry is her ability to penetrate to the heart of Aquinas's subtle and elusive discourse on *being*, and do so without the benefit of the studies cited above, indeed without much reliance on secondary literature at all. Yet her own confessed formation in the "school of Edmund Husserl . . . and phenomenological method" may have offered her a prescient optic for the potencies of Aquinas's language in trying to bring to expression this axial notion of metaphysics which in fact resists any proper conceptual formation.[2]

But let us first try to evoke the rich person of this scholar who found herself so drawn by truth as it was unveiled to her, as well as drawn to those with whom she shared this adventure: friends and students (who quickly became friends) alike. Gifted with a thoroughly intellectual temperament, her advice to a colleague, Fritz Kaufmann, reveals as well just how centered she already was at 28 (in 1919):

> I am worried at seeing how, for months, you have avoided doing purely philosophical work, and am gradually beginning to wonder whether your "profession" should not lie in a different direction. Please do not take this as a vote of "no confidence" or as doubting your ability. I only mean that one should not use force to make the center of one's life anything that fails to give one the right kind of satisfaction.[3]

Equally drawn as she was to scholarship and to guiding others to cognate goals, she could be utterly forthright in criticizing another's work, as evidenced in her response to Maria Bruck's dissertation comparing two German philosophers:

> I am convinced that if you have an opportunity to work for a few years longer at systematic philosophy, you will yourself experience the need to go beyond [this work]; not merely take an independent position on the problems you have touched but, above all, to tackle the interpretation from the basis of clearly established final principles. Without that, no actual comparison of what is meant as systematic philosophy is possible. From the start I missed a sharp delineation of what Brentano and Husserl understood as the *real* and as *essence*, and several other matters. (*SPL* #149)

To be sure, this communication begins gently: "Undoubtedly this work demanded a great deal of effort from you. It is very neat and conscientious and will surely be of lasting use for anyone who will study the relationship of Husserl to Brentano"; but its author cannot have failed to discern, in her friend Edith's words, that she had rather missed the point—philosophically.

In a more personal vein, Edith wrote to a former student who was discerning a vocation to religious life:

> God leads each of us on an individual way; one reaches the goal more easily and more quickly than another. We can do very little ourselves, compared to what is done to us. But that little bit we must do. Primarily, this consists before all else of persevering in prayer to find the right way, and of following without resistance the attraction of grace when we feel it. Whoever acts in this way and perseveres patiently will not be able to say that his efforts were in vain. But one may not set a deadline for the Lord. . . . Among the books you got as a child, do you have Andersen's Fairy Tales? If so, read the story of the ugly duckling. I believe in your swan-destiny. (*SPL* #102)

And to another former student, now teaching in school, also discerning religious life, she writes:

> To contend for souls and love them in the Lord is the Christian's duty and, actually, a special goal of the Dominican Order. But if that is your goal and if the thought of marriage is farthest from your mind, then it will be good if you soon being to wear appropriate dress. That will make it clear to people who it is they are dealing with. Otherwise there will be the danger of your misleading others, of your behavior being misinterpreted (I would be surprised if, without your being aware of it, that has not already happened at times), and your achieving exactly the opposite of what you desire. (*SPL* #103).

It should be clear how those who associated with this woman could be assured of hearing the truth as she saw it, yet at the same time many seemed ineluctably drawn to her, as she reminds her colleague Fritz (in 1931):

> The circle of persons whom I consider as connected with me has increased so much in the course of the years that it is entirely impossible to keep in touch by the usual means. But I have other ways and means of keeping the bonds alive. (*SPL* #93a)

Edith had been early on thwarted from pursuing her second doctorate (*Habilitationschrift*) for the simple reason that she was a woman, and her remarks (again to Fritz Kaufmann) on the academic politics surrounding the matter were unyielding (*SPL* #31). Yet within two weeks, she finds herself consoling him:

> It was terribly dear of you to be so zealous on my behalf, but I must tell you that things have gone very well for me in the past weeks and that I am no longer the least bit furious or sad. Instead I find the whole matter very funny. After all, I do not consider life on the whole to carry so much weight that it would matter a great deal what position I occupy. And I would like you to make that attitude your own (*SPL* #32).

She realized perfectly well that she would never be admitted to university teaching without the second doctorate, yet service was already more important than a career, so she soon immersed herself in secondary teaching at a Dominican Sisters' school in Speyer (Bavaria) soon after her baptism on 1 January 1922 (at age 31), a position she held for nine years until she resigned to complete her translation of Aquinas. All during this time she immersed herself in lectures on the place of women, especially in Catholic circles, remarking in 1931: "During my years in the *Gymnasium* and as a young student [at the university] I was a radical feminist. Then I lost interest in the whole question. Now, because I am obliged to do so, I seek purely objective solutions" (*SPL* #100).

Fully engaged in teaching young women, she made their concerns her own, yet in a quite disinterested way. This vocational commitment was, if anything, intensified in her next post at the *Deutsches Institut für Wissenschaftliche Pädagogik* (German Institute for Scientific Pedagogy), from where she continued to lecture on women's issues until 1933, when the National Socialists insisted that Jews be deprived of teaching posts. Writing again to Fritz Kaufmann, she is able to say that

> the *umsturz* was for me a sign from heaven that I might now go the way that I had long considered as mine. After a final visit with my relatives in Breslau and a difficult farewell from my dear mother, I entered the monastery of the Carmelite nuns here last Saturday and thus became a daughter of St. Teresa, who earlier inspired me to conversion. (*SPL* #158a)

In that life she would be able to pursue her interior vocation intellectually as well, and be prepared for the ultimate test, to come in less than a decade.

From what we have seen of Edith Stein, we would be hard-pressed to read her move to Carmel as "leaving the world," but rather as intensifying her presence to a world gone mad. Indeed, her letters from Breslau to her friends, on the cusp of entering Carmel, invite them all to visit her there, while reflections in an earlier (1928) letter to a Dominican sister friend help us to read the move more accurately:

> Immediately before, and for a good while after my conversion, I was of the opinion that to lead a religious life meant one had to give up all that was secular and to live totally immersed in thoughts of the Divine. But gradually I realized that something else is asked of us in this world and that, even in the contemplative life, one may not sever the connection with the world. I even believe that the deeper one is drawn into God, the more one must "go out of oneself": that is, one must go to the world in order to carry the divine life into it. The only essential is that one finds, first of all, a quiet corner in which one can communicate with God as though there

were nothing else, and that must be done daily. . . .
Furthermore, [it is essential] that one accept one's
particular mission there, preferably for each day, and not
make one's own choice. Finally, one is to consider oneself
totally as an instrument, especially with regard to the
abilities one uses to perform one's special tasks, in our
case, e.g., intellectual ones. We are to see them as
something used, not by us, but by God in us. . . . My life
begins anew each morning, and ends every evening; I have
neither plans nor prospects beyond it. (*SPL* #45)

As we shall see, it would be difficult to find a better formula for
describing a life patterned on the transformation outlined by John
of the Cross; Edith seemed to have been prepared to move quite
naturally into Sister Teresa Benedicta of the Cross.

While she did not complete her constructive monograph on
the unity of John's life and work until her final days, we can
easily discern her pull to Carmel, first in her attraction to Teresa
of Avila, and then in her inner affinity for the purity of John of
the Cross's presentation of the inner dynamics of a life of faith.
John is disarmingly forthright in identifying the goal of that
journey—"the union and transformation of the [person] in
God"—as well as the means—"faith alone, which is the only
proximate and proportionate means to union with God."[4] He is
at pains to distinguish this intentional union from the "union
between God and creatures [which] always exists [by which] God
sustains every soul and dwells in it substantially. . . . By it He
conserves their being so that if the union would end they would
immediately be annihilated and cease to exist" (*Ascent* 2.5.3).

So John will presume the unique metaphysical relation of all
creatures to their source, which Meister Eckhart elaborated from
Aquinas's distinction, and does not hesitate to call it a
union—indeed, an "essential or substantial union." This grounding
fact attends all creatures, hence it is *natural* and found in
everything (though displayed differently in animate from
inanimate, and in animate, differs from animals to humans, though
among humans it can still be found in "the greatest sinner in the
world"), while the intentional union is *supernatural* and can only

be found "where there is a likeness of love [such that] God's will and the [person's] are in conformity" (*Ascent* 2.5.3).

We shall see that what eliminates any prospect of "heteronomy" between those two wills is precisely this "non-reciprocal relation of dependence" that attends all creatures, but let us attend first to the internal connection between *faith* and *union* which John confidently asserts. What makes this sound so startling is our propensity to confine such talk to "mystics," while reducing faith to belief: holding certain propositions to be true. This is a long and complex debate in Christian theology, which often cuts oddly across confessional lines, so the best we can do here is to remind ourselves that John of the Cross could well have been responding from the Iberian peninsula to sixteenth-century winds from northern Europe. He does so by elaborating some key assertions of Aquinas to cut through the debates that polarized intellect and will in the act of faith.

First, Aquinas: "Faith is a sort of knowledge [*cognitio quaedam*] in that it makes the mind assent to something. The assent is not due to what is seen by the believer but to what is seen by him who is believed" (*Summa Theologica* 1.12.13.3). The one who is believed is, of course, the Word of God incarnate, Jesus, as mediated through the Scriptures, so this peculiar "sort of knowledge" is rooted in an interpersonal relation of the believer with Jesus. It is that relation, at the root of faith, which John of the Cross sets out to explore, quite aware that what results from it will "fall short of the mode of knowing [*cognitio*] which is properly called 'knowledge' [*scientia*], for such knowledge causes the mind to assent through what is seen and through an understanding of first principles."

More positively, Aquinas will characterize faith as "an act of mental assent commanded by the will, [so] to believe perfectly our mind must tend unfailingly towards the perfection of truth, in unfailing service of that ultimate goal for the sake of which our will is commanding our mind's assent" (*ST* 2-2.4.5). Unlike ordinary belief, then, faith must be an act of the whole person, involving a personal and critical quest for a truth that outreaches our proper expression. John will focus critically on our concepts: "nothing which could possibly be imagined or comprehended in this life can be a proximate means of union with God" (*ST* 2.8.4), since "nothing created or imagined can serve the intellect as a proper means for union with God; [indeed], all that can be grasped by the intellect would serve as an obstacle rather than a means, if a person were to become attached to it" (*ST* 2.8.1). So following Aquinas, we must be able to let our conceptualties "lead us on by the hand" [*manuductio*], as John does, to a goal that transcends them. That goal, we recall, is "union and transformation of the [person] in God," and it is already intimated in the sort of *faith* of which Thomas and John are speaking.

As Augustine had already worked it out, Christian faith differs from ordinary belief in being a response to an utterly gratuitous invitation, which could never be initiated by persons themselves. So this treatment of faith and union anticipates the critiques of both Freud and Marx, while leaving room for both. For if Freud would reduce religious faith to projections, Aquinas will also insist that "faith that does not rely on divine truth can fail and believe falsehood" (*ST* 2-2.4.5), yet if we regard John of the Cross as developing Aquinas's lapidary exposition of faith, authentic faith will ever involve a journey of responding rather than initiating, with intervening projections being submitted to a searing critique.

And with regard to Marx, it is John's forthright insistence on union that responds to Marx's characterization of Christian faith as alienating human beings from their authentic life and work by offering a distracting "heavenly reward," for the union of which John speaks begins now. Yet Marx's account may well address a Christian ethos quite innocent of the tradition, which John articulates, of an internal connection between faith and union, so Marx's critique can well fuel the kind of internal critique that John's account of faith demands. Indeed, the demands of that journey of faith which John outlines are utterly rigorous: "We shall explain how in order to journey to God the intellect must be perfected in the darkness of faith, the memory in the emptiness of hope, and the will in the nakedness and absence of every affection [unrelated to the goal of union]" (*ST* 2.6.1).

A poetic characterization of that intentional union is offered in his "Living Flame of Love," where we can compare the initial stanza of the poem together with statements from his own commentary:

O living flame of love
That tenderly wounds my soul
In its deepest center! Since
Now You are not oppressive,
Now Consummate! If it be your will:
Tear through the veil of this sweet encounter!

The commentary begins:

The soul now feels that it all inflamed in the divine union,
. . . and that in the most intimate part of its substance it is
flooded with no less than rivers of glory, abounding in
delights, and that from its bosom flow rivers of living waters
[Jn 7:38], which the Son of God declared will rise up in such
souls. Accordingly it seems, because it is so vigorously transformed in God, so sublimely possessed by Him, and arrayed
with such rich gifts and virtues, that it is singularly close to
beatitude—so close that only a thin veil separates it. (1.1)

He continues:

This flame of love is the Spirit of the Bridegroom, which
is the Holy Spirit. . . . Such is the activity of the Holy
Spirit in the soul transformed in love: the interior acts He
produces shoot up flames for they are acts of inflamed
love, in which the will of the soul united with that flame,
made one with it, loves most sublimely. . . . Thus in this
state the soul cannot make acts because the Holy Spirit
makes them all and moves it towards them. As a result all
the acts of the soul are divine, since the movement toward
these acts and their execution stems from God. Hence it
seems to a person that every time this flame shoots up,
making him love with delight and divine quality, it is
giving him eternal life, since it raises him up to the
activity of God in God. (1.3-4)

There is no hint of "heteronomy" here, I would suggest, because
John presumes that unique metaphysical relation of person

("soul") to its source, which Meister Eckhart had developed from Aquinas.

Sister Teresa Benedicta had become attuned to that unique relation of creatures to their creator in her study of Aquinas on eternal and temporal being, which led her into the presence of the great mystery of creation:

> that God has called forth each being into its differentiated being; a manifold of beings in which what is one in God is there separate. . . . [Yet] the subsistence of creatures is no longer that of a portrait over against the one portrayed, or of a work over against the artist doing it. Earlier [thinkers] had likened the relation to that of a mirror to the object in the mirror, or of refracted light to its pure source, yet these remain but imperfect images for what is quite incomparable. (*EES* 320-21)

She then goes on to compare the creator/creature relation to the relations among the divine "persons":

> The entire divine essence is common to all three persons. So what remains is simply the differences of the persons as such: a perfect unity of *we*, which no community of finite persons could ever realize, yet in this unity the difference of *I* from *you* remains, without which no *we* is possible. . . . Indeed, the *we* as the unity of *I* and *you*—"I and the Father are one" (Jo 10:30)—is a higher unity than the *I*. For in its most perfect sense, it is the unity of love. Now love as assent to a good is possible as the self-love of an *I*, but love is more than such an assent, more than a "valuing." It is gift of oneself to the *thou*, and in its perfection—on the strength of manifold gifts of self—an existential unity [*Einssein*]. Since God is love, divine being must be an existential unity of a multiplicity of persons, while the divine name "I am" is identical in meaning with "I give myself totally to you," "I am one with a *you*," and so also identical with "we are." The love of the life interior to God can never be replaced, however, by the

love between God and creatures, which can never attain love in its highest perfection—even when it be realized in the richest perfection of glory. For the highest love is differentiated eternal love: God loves creatures from eternity, whereas God can never be loved by them from eternity. (*EES* 323-24)

So while the *we* of human lovers may offer an image for divine triunity, it will always fall short of that eternal unity; yet the very relation of creatures to creator defies representation, so the unity with God to which humans can be elevated by grace must be likened to that within the triune God, even though the one can never replace the other. What is incomparable can nonetheless be compared. That is the paradox into which the analogical metaphysics of Aquinas invites us, and to which the poetic genius of John of the Cross will give its most proper expression. For his poetry gives voice to the utterly unique "distinction" of creatures from creator, which we have seen John already calling a "union" in the nature of created things with their creator, and one which becomes intentionally so in those who permit the interior transformation by the Holy Spirit into "images of god" become "images of Christ." In this way the circumincession of human and divine that characterizes Jesus can be bestowed upon human agents who have been turned into lovers.

So Edith Stein, become Sister Teresa Benedicta of the Cross, traced the divine becoming so aptly described by John of the Cross in her life and works, as he had limned it in his, so that her apprenticeship to him reflects ours to them both, in the circumincession of emulation which characterizes a community of revelation, as friendships sustain each of us in our search for Truth as we attempt to incorporate that Truth into the truth of our lives.

Notes

1. St. John of the Cross, *The Spiritual Canticle*, in *The Collected Works of St. John of the Cross*, ed. Kiernan Kavanaugh and Otilio Rodriguez (Washington: ICS Publishers, 1991), xxi.

2. Edith Stein, *Endliches und Ewiges Sein* (Leuven: Nauwelaerts/ Freiburg: Herder, 1950), viii. Cited hereafter in the text of my essay as *EES* followed by page number.

3. Edith Stein, *Self-Portrait in Letters*, ed. L. Gelber and Romaeus Leuven, translated by Josephine Koeppel (Washington: Institute of Carmelite Studies, 1993), #29a. Cited hereafter in the text of my essay as *SPL*.

4. St. John of the Cross, *Ascent of Mount Carmel*, 2.5.3; 2.9.1. Cited hereafter in the text of my essay as *Ascent*, followed by section and chapter number.

Living the Gospel
in Today's Unforgiving World

CAMILLE D'ARIENZO

I would like to begin by thanking Father Martin and this Benedictine community for inviting me to deliver one of their jubilee presentations. Mount Saviour's jubilee coincides with my golden jubilee as a Sister of Mercy. This monastery for more than half my religious life has nurtured my soul and I always experience a sense of homecoming in this homeland of my heart.

My other home, the convent in which I live with three other sisters in Glendale, Queens, has a flat roof from which I can see the Manhattan skyline. It is hard to look at the void where the twin towers stood until September 11. My two nephews, both New York City policemen, have spent the weeks since then sifting through the rubble left by the terrorists. Some of the rubble was human remains. All over were the ashes of incinerated innocent men, women, and children. Michael and Ronnie had a separate agenda: they were searching for their lost cousin, an electrician employed at the site, a good and decent man who left a wife, a toddler, and an infant.

It is impossible to ignore the consequences of that attack in a presentation about forgiveness and reconciliation. That event has been part of talks on numerous subjects. The highly respected public broadcaster Bill Moyers justified its inclusion in a keynote address before an Environmental Grantmakers Association on October 16. Moyers acknowledged that the events of September 11 have changed us all. He says that they will unite Americans in the same way Pearl Harbor did his parents' generation. For people of his generation and mine it was the assassinations of the Kennedys and Martin Luther King, the dogs and fire hoses in Alabama.

Moyers explains: "For this generation, that [defining] moment will be September 11, 2001—the worst act of terrorism in our nation's history. It has changed the country. It has changed us." He continues:

> That's what terrorists intend. Terrorists don't want to own our land, wealth, monuments, buildings, fields, or streams. They're not after tangible property. Sure, they aim to annihilate the targets they strike. But their real goal is to get inside our heads, our psyche, and to deprive us—the survivors—of peace of mind, of trust, of faith; they aim to prevent us from believing again in a world of mercy, justice, and love, or working to bring that better world to pass.

"This is their real target," he adds, "to turn our imaginations into Afghanistans, where they can rule by fear. Once they possess us, they are hard to exorcise."

Like many thoughtful people, I long for justice for the perpetrators of the attack, but not for a war inflicted on innocent civilians. And I pray for ways to resist inflicting the kind of violence that could transform us into the enemy we despise. This desire is what draws us to communities of faith where we can find direction and support for the lessons learned from Jesus Christ, the Prince of Peace. As we come with this common wound inflicted on September 11, we come also with our personal hurts. We look for ways to prevent them from becoming cancers in our souls.

It is with a mix of trepidation and inner peace that I dare to address today's topic: Living the Gospel in Today's Unforgiving World. I have been around long enough to have experienced personally and vicariously a wide range of miseries. I have marveled at the capacity of some people to overcome evil with goodness. Conversely, I have seen the intensification of suffering that occurs in those who cannot let go of the griefs and injustices that have bruised and battered them.

My desire is to examine those circumstances and actions that wound us, to consider the limits and possibilities of forgiveness, the nature and consequences of reconciliation, and the struggle to be faithful in an environment that considers this enterprise naïve or foolish. I will share what I have learned from others, from the deep reservoir of faith, and from life. I will draw on stories, all true, that have formed my thinking. I invite you to accept what is useful or productive for your own spiritual development and to cast aside that which is useless and to forgive my limitations.

I begin with the blessed words God spoke through the prophet Isaiah, words that are breathtakingly beautiful, emotionally stirring, intellectually compelling. God asks:

> Is this not the sort of fast that pleases me—
> it is the Lord Yahweh who speaks—
> to loose the bonds of injustice,
> to undo the thongs of the yoke,
> to let the oppressed go free,
> to share your bread with the hungry,
> and shelter the homeless poor,
> to clothe the one you see to be naked
> and not turn from your own kin?
> Then will your light shine like the dawn
> And your wound be quickly healed over.
> (Isaiah 58:6-10)

Isaiah's values are the values Jesus embodied. They are the goals of his followers. They are beautiful to consider and difficult to apply in a world so often wounded and wounding. God promises that when we immerse ourselves in the concerns of others, our own wounds will be healed; however, we often need to work on ourselves before we can enter the sufferings of others.

As pilgrims and searchers we struggle to find authentic places where we can bring our deepest hurts and find the spiritual and psychic energy to shed the chains that bind us, to shake the oppression that keeps us from freedom of mind and heart. It is amazing how many of us are impelled to share those sacred places we carve out for ourselves with those we care about. Centuries ago, Seneca, pondering the grandeur of the earth, the splendor of a sunset, described his urgency to share his discoveries with others. He concluded:

Even the best and most useful gives me no pleasure if I alone may know it. If all that is best and beautiful were offered to me on the condition that I keep it hoarded up within my own soul and share it with no one, I would refuse it. We cannot enjoy a treasure without a companion to our joy.

For many of us, Mount Saviour Monastery has been a treasure we have been compelled to share with others. My guess is that most, if not all, have told others about this holy mountain and have invited them to see for themselves what we cherish and to find for themselves what they need.

Twenty years ago, *Mount Saviour Chronicle*, marking the fifteen hundredth anniversary of the birth of St. Benedict and the thirtieth of this monastery, carried an expression of appreciation for the hospitality discovered here. At that time I wrote:

> We who come here walk through many worlds. We're college professors and laborers, educated and unlettered, rich and poor, broken and healers, and, as the late Henri Nouwen put it, "wounded healers." We're celibate and wondering if we've really served the Lord in our barrenness. We're married and anxious that we've not sufficiently prepared the children we've brought into the world. We're young and restless, old and discouraged. We're young and discouraged, old and restless.

> We come, for the most part, as strangers, bonded only by the qualities that draw us like magnets to this monastery. . . . This monastery, your community of Benedictines, acts as a kind of centrifugal force that pulls us to seek God. We come in search of a credible evidence of faith from which we can draw strength and encouragement.

> What we find in you is openness and easy hospitality. We find more. We find constancy—a handful of men who in good times and bad praise God, in the presence of outsiders, in the privacy of community.

> You may think of yourselves as weak, imperfect, tired, discouraged, anxious, at odds with one another . . . less

than exquisitely successful. You may be all that, but you are real. The regularity of your lives, the predictability of your prayer is a sign of God's fidelity to all creation, to each of us who live today and come to you because we thirst for living waters. You speak to us of Jesus Christ and image him in the fidelity of your lives. You help contemporize the Gospel message. You compensate for much of what is weak and shallow in the Church. You support many who are good and who want to be better, many who are weak and long to be strong.

Wisdom teaches that joy is an infallible sign of the presence of God. So many times good humor has burst forth in the midst of monastic trials. Some years ago, I recall, word was out that the crypt at the monastery was flooded. Fixing the problem would be costly. My local convent sent a small donation. The response came on a postcard from Father Martin. His physician's scrawl, deciphered, read: "Thanks for your contribution. That entitles you to one canoe ride in our crypt."

Old photographs, going back to 1975, remind me of the women and men I have transported. On a wall in our convent is one of Brother Luke's original paintings. It is a gift from a man I brought here more than twenty years ago because I didn't have sufficient strength to help him myself. I will call him John Ellison.

John was a brilliant, thoroughly eccentric teacher in my department at Brooklyn College. He lived in Greenwich Village with a talented photographer about half his age. John was estranged from the church; Brad had no religious connections. One terrible night Brad committed suicide. John went berserk. I helped as much as I could, identifying the body at the morgue, preparing a funeral service held at the crematorium on a dark December day.

John's behavior deteriorated. He frightened his students and was in jeopardy of losing his position. I didn't know what drove him. I think guilt, a sense of abandonment, and fury at God were part of the mix. He agreed to let me bring him here for a week during winter break. I thought he might find solace in the services and solitude. In fact, he came to few services. He spent a lot of time with the cows the monastery then had and a great deal of time with the late Brother Ansgar. One or the other, or both, restored his sanity. He got on with his life—never fully healed, but relieved of the consuming anger that would have destroyed him. Brother Luke's painting holds that memory and my gratitude.

Were all our individual stories compiled, they would rise like incense from the sacrificial lives of the monks who make a place for us here.

There are, of course, many people we would like to bring here, and can't. It is possible that we may *become* the places accessible to them, that we may be the ambassadors of peace and mercy, healing others' wounds. And yet, before we behave expansively, we must be introspective. We bear the wounds of our hurts, from wrongs inflicted from the outside, but also from our own sins, private or public.

I invite you to enter into a moment of silence. Recall, if you dare, your most humiliating experience—shameful because you committed the deed. How did you handle it? How long were you able to conceal it? Is it resolved today in your human family? Have you been honest and fair about it? How would you feel if that sorry affair became the news of the day? Suppose that and that alone were the matter by which you were known and judged?

The prophet Jeremiah reminds us that "More devious than all else is the human heart . . . who can understand it?" (Jeremiah 17:8). Only when our shameful deeds are forgiven can our "wound be healed over." Who does the forgiving? In his homily last Sunday, Father Martin drew from the sixty-second psalm, reminding us that God's love is greater than life. Surely we long for forgiveness from the God of the prodigal family, the God who never tires of waiting for our return, who knows we can repent and reform and grow in grace and spiritual beauty. We learn from that parable to extend the same attitudes to others.

Some thirty years ago I learned the power of that attitude from a tearful woman in St. Cecilia's Church in Detroit. Its vibrant, charismatic forty-seven-year-old pastor, Father Ray Ellis, had died of a heart attack. He was significantly important in that city and his death was the lead story on the evening news. The woman, like myself, had immediately headed for the church. As

I was leaving, overwhelmed by the testimonies of that black congregation, I found her trembling and weeping in the vestibule. "I want to go to his coffin, she said, but I can't like this." She wore a strapless red mini-dress, leaving little doubt as to her profession. I lent her my jacket and when she returned it she spoke words that sank deep into my heart: "He was the only man who ever thought I could be more than what I am."

Somewhere in the formula for forgiveness there ought to be an expectation, an encouragement for the offenders, ourselves included, to be more than what they are. We also need to beg forgiveness of ourselves and of those whom we have hurt or betrayed. Sometimes it is too late for the latter. How do we then enter into God's generous economy to make restitution in some alternative way?

The sacrament of reconciliation invites us to a homecoming, to return to God with our whole hearts. Christ's gift of redemption is about giving sinners, ourselves included, a second chance to live. The parable of the Prodigal Son consoles us with the message that God's love far exceeds our capacity to sin. We believe in God's forgiving love more than we do our ability to emulate it.

An old woman I know once asked, "Who wrote the Our Father?" I explained as best I could. She countered, "Whoever wrote it down got it wrong. It is too hard to forgive. Jesus would never expect that of us." For many, it is too hard to forgive unaided. The psalmist reminds us, however, "God draws near to all who call on God." It is another reason we seek community. This person has something in common with unhappy people I have known in all walks of life: a refusal to relinquish the hurts of her life. In the childhood she shared with eight other siblings, she alone remembers relentless poverty. Despite trips and parties and holidays prepared by family members, she insists she has never had a happy day in her life. Out of her rage have come numerous prescriptions for causing unhappiness in the lives of others. She has no friends. The anger and discontent by which she has defined herself prevent her from enjoying the present or planning the future. She continues to give power to yesterday's evils. We see this situation in many families whose members refuse to speak to one another, to resolve the issues of alienation.

Two weeks ago today, the Cherish Life Circle, which we established to address the painful issue of capital punishment, hosted its fourth annual service for families and friends of murder victims. About two hundred people, representing thirty families, attended the interfaith candlelight service in Our Lady of Refuge Church in Brooklyn. Father Michael Perry is pastor there and a member of our Cherish Life Circle.

One family that came early and from some distance consisted of a husband and wife in their late fifties and a boy of about ten. Over refreshments he told me his story: Four years earlier his twenty-six-year-old son, Kenny, had been shot to death. Kenny's brother, unable to cope with the death, has become a street person. A few weeks after the murder a woman from the south appeared at the couple's door with a child of six she said was Kenny's son. They didn't know they were grandparents. She didn't know Kenny had died. Two months later she was murdered. The child they brought with them was an orphan, having lost both parents to killers.

This grandfather who was raising the boy had suffered a stroke. He said he and his wife can barely cope. They haven't celebrated a single holiday since their son was killed. He said, "The stranger who murdered my son killed our whole family."

Sometimes grieving for a lost child or parent or spouse can be the stone at the door to the heart that locks in the love required by the living, like the ten-year-old boy. It is clear that until that desolate man can let go of the suffering, he will continue to increase it in his life and the lives of those he cares about.

This situation only hints at the complexity of forgiveness. Permit me now to share my perceptions, fallible and incomplete, on the nature of forgiveness, its context and implications, and the limits of forgiveness. Forgiveness is not abstract, disconnected. It is rooted in pain, injustice, loss, and a sense of betrayal, abandonment. Are there limits to forgiveness? I think so—at least to a person's right to forgive. It is insensitive to suggest that we must all forgive everybody everything. If someone kills your best friend, I have no right to forgive that killer.

I hope the following story will provoke some serious thinking. I draw from the core of Simon Wiesenthal's book, *The*

Sunflower. Simon Wiesenthal was a prisoner in Nazi concentration camps during the Holocaust years. The title of the book comes from his memories of rows upon rows of sunflowers in a cemetery where German soldiers were buried. Jews he knew who died in the gas ovens, including all the members of his own family, had no definable resting place, no tombstones, no sunflowers. The story has five elements: a prisoner, a dying man, the context, the evil and the response.

While imprisoned in a Nazi concentration camp, Wiesenthal was taken one day from his work disposing of medical waste at a hospital, to the bedside of a tortured, dying Nazi soldier. The young patient's face was wrapped in bandages. Only his eyes showed and they were haunted by his crimes. In the absence of a priest, the soldier wanted to confess to—and obtain absolution from—a Jew.

Wiesenthal was at the bedside under protest. The soldier described the way he and his comrades had herded a large number of Jews into a building, locked the doors and set it ablaze. Trapped inside were women and children and old people.

"Forgive me," the dying man implored.

Struggling with his own rage, an appalled Wiesenthal said nothing. Back at the camp, he argued the matter with other prisoners. Years after the war had ended, Wiesenthal wondered if he had done the right thing.

What would you have done? Plagued by uncertainty, Wiesenthal includes in his book responses from fifty-three individuals: theologians, political leaders, jurists, psychiatrists, human rights activists, and victims of genocide in Bosnia, Cambodia, China, and Tibet.

One response credible to me was this: "I don't have it in my power or heart to forgive you. Throw yourself on the mercy of God in whom you believe. Ask God's forgiveness."

Hans Habe, a Hungarian reporter and newspaper editor during the Holocaust years said, "Forgiveness is the imitation of God. Punishment, too, is in imitation of God. God punishes and forgives, in that order. But God never hates." Those last three words speak volumes to me. "God never hates." Not hating implies creating an environment where the offender can pursue virtue if he chooses. Not hating means removing obstacles to reformation.

There is a second part to that story. The dying soldier asked the prisoner to deliver a letter to his mother back in Germany, if the prisoner survived the death camp. Months later, Wiesenthal carried the letter to the German mother. He may have intended to reveal his hatred of her son and the deeds he perpetrated as a soldier. However, when he found the widow, grieving for her only son, living in postwar squalor, with little understanding of what happened, he could not hurt her more. He pretended to have received that letter from someone who had met her son. In fact, he again chose silence.

For the purpose of this reflection, I offer the dictionary's definition of forgiveness: 1) to give up resentment against or the desire to punish, stop being angry with; pardon; 2) to give up all claim to punish or exact penalty for an offense; 3) to cancel a debt.

How many times can we do this? Seventy times seven?

Forgiveness sets the sinner free. It also frees the forgiver from lugging around the burden of anger. It allows her to devote her energies to worthier enterprises.

We are all wounded people. Who wounds us? Often those we love, those who love us. At times we feel abandoned, betrayed. Why weren't you there for me?

Forgiveness does not mean forgetting. The memory, even the wound may stay forever. How do we forgive parents who have abused us? How do children forgive their parents for divorcing, or parents their children who have betrayed their values? How do people forgive doctors for their bad advice, friends for their insensitivity to our suffering? How do we forgive God for the death of a loved one or a crippling disease?

The way in which we cope with suffering alters us, making us stronger or weaker. Many of us know the story of the poet Maya Angelou. When she was six, she was raped and hurt and hospitalized. She knew her attacker and identified him. He was captured, jailed, and released. The next day his body was discovered. He had been beaten to death. Now the young Maya blamed herself for her rapist's death because she had spoken his name. At that point she stopped speaking. For the next six years she read everything she could get her hands on. She memorized the works of the great poets, all of Shakespeare's sonnets. When she decided to use her voice again she had much to say and the tools with which to say it. In a symposium on the problem of evil hosted by Bill Moyers some years ago, she shared this story and her formula for self healing: "Name the evil, forgive it, and let it go."

How does one forgive a murderer? Some cannot. Some, like Bud Welch, who lost his twenty-three-year-old daughter Julie in the Oklahoma City bombing, had to, both to honor his daughter's memory and to save himself from self-destruction by rage. Bud Welch's public forgiveness of Timothy McVeigh had an impact on Patrick Reeder, who lost his wife in that 1995 bombing.

For months he harbored consuming hatred and a desire to kill the bomber himself. He could think of no other goal. He lost an enormous amount of weight, turned to drink and disruptive, violent behavior. Bud Welch's comments in the media first disgusted, and then challenged him. Mr. Reeder felt himself in a black hole of rage and revenge and sorrow. He told the *New York Times*, "I was turning into a beast. I started to think, Who is a better person, McVeigh or me?"

In the end, Reeder was one of the few of his family members who opposed McVeigh's execution last June. He remained bothered by the bomber's lack of remorse. He believes, however, that executing him removes the impetus to examine his own complex feelings about justice and forgiveness. He said he understood the desire of many to eliminate McVeigh, adding, "I felt that way myself. I wanted him silenced. But I also wanted my own conscience silenced."

Let me tell you about Marietta Jaegher Lane. More than twenty years ago she was with her family in a camping trip in her home state of Montana. One night while all were asleep, someone cut a hole in the tent and snatched her seven-year-old daughter, Susie. A massive search yielded no clues. After about six months Marietta had a dream, which convinced her that her little girl was in heaven. Six months later, on the first anniversary of the abduction, she received a taunting call from the abductor. He told her he was holding her daughter captive and was teaching her to forget her family. Marietta, who had accepted the child's death and prayed for the gift of forgiveness, gently asked, "How can I help you?" The caller hung up and Marietta reported the call to the police.

Encouraged by her sympathy the man called back, allowing the police to trace the call and to capture the killer. The twenty-eight-year-old Vietnam veteran had taken the little girl to an abandoned farmhouse where he kept her locked in a closet, sexually molested her, killed her, and ate some of her flesh. Only by offering that description can I convey Marietta's incredible courage. She did not have a chance to forgive the man because he committed suicide in prison. But she had to forgive him for her own sake. This is her explanation: "Forgiveness is a letting go of the desire for punishment and, instead, taking up the idea of restoration, of putting things back in some good order, although it might not be the same order." "Forgiveness," she adds, "means feeling concern, even love for the offender."

Today Marietta Jaegher Lane is a prominent member of Families of Murder Victims for Reconciliation. Like you, I marvel at her capacity for forgiveness. There is nothing more personal than the murder of a loved one.

Many of the evils we experience are communal, societal. We suffer and react as part of a group or nation. Vietnamese Zen Master Thich Nhat Hanh suggests a way of proceeding:

> Reconciliation is to understand both sides, to go to one side and describe the suffering being endured by that side; then to go to the other side and describe the suffering endured by the first side.

Abraham Heschel reminds us of another dimension. The prophet, he says, has to see human experience from God's point of view. Since Cain slew Abel, individuals and nations have resorted to violence to eliminate threats or competition or settle disputes. Most claim the right to do this, based on the perils and exigencies of any given time.

Here in Mark Twain country I am reminded of the wisdom of that author's remarkable parable published, at his request, after his death. It is called *The War Prayer*, a work he created in 1923.

The book is out of print now, but the Steele Memorial Library has two copies. Twain sets it in the context of patriotic fervor attending the start of a war. The parish church is filled to overflowing with citizens proud of their young men's willingness to defend their country. Their minister leads them in a rallying prayer for victory. He concludes, eyes closed with these words:

> O Lord, our Father, our young and patriotic idols
> Of our hearts go forth to battle; be Thou near them.
> With them in spirit we also go from the sweet peace
> Of our beloved firesides to smite the foe.

When he opens his eyes, he finds before him an ancient, dark robed man, who cautions the congregation to beware of what they pray for. With each prayer, there is a shadow one. He intones the minister's unspoken second prayer. Here are some excerpts:

> O Lord our God, help us to tear their soldiers to bloody
>   shreds
> with our shells;
> help us to drown the thunder of the guns
> with the shrieks of their wounded,
> writhing in pain;
> help us lay waste their humble homes
> with a hurricane of fire;
> help us to wring the hearts of their unoffending widows
> with unavailing grief;
> help us to turn them out roofless,
> with their little children to wander unfriended the wastes
> of their desolated land in rags and hunger and thirst,

And so it continues through a host of images, and then:

> We ask this in the spirit of love,
> Who is the Source of Love and who is the ever
> Faithful refuge and friend of all that are sore beset
> And seek His aid with humble and contrite hearts. Amen.

The old man then dares the congregation to pray the pastor's prayer now if they can. And he leaves the church. The story concludes, "It was believed afterward that the man was a lunatic because there was no sense it what he said."

In our own real world, it is often true that we who seek and extend forgiveness, who encourage reconciliation in families and among nations, who believe in the limitless possibilities of redemption and repentance, and alternatives to violence, are also believed to be less than sane. As we recognize the affliction of being harshly judged, we can realize that our own harsh judgments can be impediments to reconciliation.

This presentation began with a tribute to the hospitality of Mount Saviour and the need for us to create safe and healing places. In fact, to sometimes be those places where people can come for solace. I wouldd like to tell you about two children, both ten years old, one wearing brown shoes; the other with blood on his sneakers.

The first is a boy in brown shoes. He came hesitantly into the vestibule of the big Brooklyn church where we held our first service for families of murder victims. The boy was dressed in his Sunday best—right down to shoes, instead of sneakers. Thinking he was in the wrong place, I asked him why he had come.

"My mama sent me," he said. She had heard that morning about the service and couldn't come herself, so he came to represent the family. His fifteen-year-old brother had been murdered a few weeks earlier. Someone hastily wrote his brother's name on eight-and-a-half-by-eleven cards, which he, like the others, wore around his neck. We put him in a pew with some mothers.

After hymns, a scripture reading and a reflection by a woman whose son had been murdered, we called the names on the cards. Each bearer came forth, lit his or her candle from the Paschal candle, and formed a semi-circle in the sanctuary. When the little guy's brother's name was called, he walked out of the pew bravely, and then his shoulders crumpled and he started to cry as the mothers embraced him. What that child learned that day was the supportive, loving faith of a community of understanding and solace. This was a gathering devoid of calls for violence or vengeance. After the service, everyone retired to the basement for refreshments. I looked for the child, but he had disappeared. He remains a reminder of the legacy of faith and forgiveness we owe our children.

And now the boy with blood on his shoes. He and his brother and sister suffered vicious psychological and sexual abuse at the hands of their drug-addicted, transient parents. One day a kind aunt gave the ten-year-old a puppy. Immediately the children bonded with the mutt. When their mother discovered the puppy, she put it in a burlap bag and as the children looked on, clubbed it to death. Then as the boy sobbed, she forced him to drag the bag to the river and dump the corpse. That's how the blood got on his sneakers.

I don't know the name of the boy in brown shoes, but I do know the boy who had blood on his sneakers. His name is David Paul Hammer. By the time the boy, David, was sixteen, he was a drug addict bent on a life of crime. At nineteen he went to jail for armed robbery and attempted murder. With the exception of two jailbreaks, he has been incarcerated ever since. He is now forty-three and anticipating execution on death row in Terre Haute, Indiana. He came, uninvited, into my life three years ago and has changed me forever.

During the 1993 New York State gubernatorial race, in which the restoration of the death penalty was a key issue, a small group of us sisters, priests, and lay people formed a Cherish Life Circle. Our goal was to pray together and provide opportunities to examine the difficult issue of capital punishment. We wanted to add to the public discourse the gifts of civility, respect, and the teachings of Jesus. We circulated a Declaration of Life. That document says that if the signer is murdered, he or she does not want his or her killer executed. The Declaration is a catalyst for conversation. Many thousands have signed it.

Every few years some newspaper reporter finds it intriguing and does an article, which is widely circulated. David read about it in 1998. His letter began, "Dear Cherish Life Circle. My name is David Paul Hammer. I'm scheduled to be executed by the federal government on January 14, 1999. I am looking for someone to pray for me and my victim, Andrew Marti, and for the Marti family. I would like someone to serve as a spiritual adviser for the final weeks of my life."

I had never visited a prisoner. I had no desire to do so. I'm an academic. I wanted to write and talk about the death penalty. It was shortly before Christmas. No one seemed able to visit him. I went to Allenwood Penitentiary in Pennsylvania where he was. Soon after, David received a stay of execution and was transferred to Terre Haute.

With God's grace and the encouragement of others, David has confessed, repented, and is attempting some sort of restitution by raising money to help abused children. The Christmas cards in the portery are his effort, with my support, to do that. He knows, as does Marietta Jaegher, that it is impossible to change the past or restore the shattered order of things. He can only sow some seeds of love where hatred had reigned.

The death penalty, of course, would be the topic of another talk. I will say here only that I recognize the difficulty this issue poses for good people, including family members closest to me. I understand well the words that Jesus spoke to Peter in John's Gospel: "When you were young, you girded yourself and went where you chose to go. When you are old, another will lead you to places you'd not have chosen."

At this time, the Supreme Court has rejected all of David's appeals. He anticipates a 2002 execution date. At his request, I will be with him when he dies. That will be the hardest thing I have ever done. I have witnessed his conversion, his entrance into the Catholic Church last year, his confirmation and first communion, all on death row in Terre Haute, Indiana, in the presence of Archbishop Buechlein. It was the first Mass celebrated in Terre Haute's Death Row. The four men who attended looked out from separate cages, into which the Eucharistic Lord entered.

One final, somewhat related story. For the past seven years, I have begged family and friends to honor my October birthday by giving me men's white socks wrapped in Christmas paper. One of our sisters, Mary O'Connor, is a longtime chaplain in the Men's House at Rikers. She used to use her allowance to provide socks to the many who attend Midnight Mass. I usually help her distribute them. Last year a photographer came. On Christmas Day the *Daily News* carried a large photo of Mary handing a prisoner a package, with me looking on. One of my policeman nephews had something to say about it on Christmas. These are Michael's words: "We're some family, Aunt Camille. I send them to Rikers and you give them socks." So in our diversity, in our varied experiences, we struggle to be faithful to the words of Isaiah, which hold a formula in a love song to heal our wounds.

In conclusion, I believe:

We must be willing to name the evil that afflicts us, realizing that, to ignore or adhere to it gives continuing power to the person or evil that wounded us to begin with us.

Some sins are inexcusable.

There are some sins that we don't have the power to forgive. Only God has that power.

Our challenge is to learn from and move away from the sins that wound us.

Out of our efforts to remain faithful to God's redemptive love, we try to encourage other sinners to have faith, to reform their lives, and to replace evil with goodness.

Finally, I believe in a just and merciful God, a God who punishes and forgives, but never hates. It is in this manner that we are challenged to love God and our neighbor.

And then, only then, will our own wounds be healed.

Contributors

MARTIN BOLER, O.S.B., is a priest and Prior of Mount Saviour Monastery in Pine City, New York, an autonomous community of monks living a full monastic life according to the Scriptures and the *Rule of St. Benedict*.

DAVID B. BURRELL, C.S.C., is a priest and Professor of Philosophy and Theology at the University of Notre Dame. With a Ph.D. from Yale, he has been teaching philosophy and theology for thirty years, has taught in Jerusalem, Cairo and Bangladesh, and explores philosophical theology in Judaism, Christianity, and Islam.

ANTHONY J. CERNERA, Ph.D., is President of Sacred Heart University, Fairfield, Connecticut. He earned a Doctorate of Philosophy in Systematic Theology from Fordham University and has promoted international symposia and edited several books on the Catholic Intellectual Tradition.

MARY COLLINS, O.S.B., Ph.D., is Prioress of the Benedictine Sisters at Mount Saint Scholastica, in Atchison, Kansas. A feminist theologian, she has chaired the religion departments at The Catholic University of America, University of Kansas at Lawrence, and the Benedictine College, Atchison, Kansas. Among her publications are "Women at Prayer, Worship: Renewal to

Practice" and "Contemplative Participation: *Sacrosanctum Concilium* Twenty-Five Years Later."

CAMILLE D'ARIENZO, R.S.M., is a Sister of Mercy from Brooklyn. An Adjunct Professor of Public Speaking at the College of Professional Studies, St. John's University, she founded the Cherish Life Circle group, and is dedicated to the abolition of the death penalty in the U.S.

JEREMY DRISCOLL, O.S.B., S.T.D., is a Benedictine monk and a priest at Mount Angel Abbey in Oregon. He also teaches theology at Mount Angel Seminary and at the Pontifical Athanaeum San Anselmo in Rome. His main fields of academic interest are Patristics and Liturgical Theology.

CHARLES DUMONT, O.C.S.O., is a Cistercian monk and priest of Notre-Dame de Scourmont Abbey in Belgium. Editor of *Collectanea Cisterciensia*, he helped establish the English counterpart, *Cistercian Studies*. He has written extensively on Saint Bernard of Clairvaux.

FRANK T. GRISWOLD is Presiding Bishop of the Episcopal Church USA. With degrees from Harvard and Oxford University, he is lead pastor and chief administrator of the 2.3 million-member Episcopal Church USA. He was formerly Bishop of Chicago, and has two adult daughters.

MARIE JULIANNE FARRINGTON, S.S.M.N., is the former general of the Sisters of St. Mary of Namur. Her community has many houses in Rwanda, and she has spoken out against the injustices there on many occasions.

TIMOTHY KELLY, O.S.B., is the ninth abbot of Saint John's Abbey, Collegeville, Minnesota. A teacher of English and theology, and on the Board of the U.S. Catholic China Bureau, he is president of the American-Cassinese Congregation of Benedictine Monasteries of Men.

JEROME KODELL, O.S.B., is abbot of the Benedictine Subiaco Abbey in Arkansas, which originated from the Abbey of Maria-Einsiedeln in Switzerland.

GOTTFRIED BURKHARD NEUNHEUSER, O.S.B., died ·at Maria Laach Abbey, Germany, in November 2003 shortly before his one hundredth birthday. An expert in Dom Odo Casel's "mystery theology," he taught liturgy at San Anselmo in Rome for decades.

JOHN T. NOONAN, JR., Ph.D., U.S. Circuit Judge, joined the Notre Dame Center for Ethics and Culture during his tenure as a visiting professor at the Notre Dame Law School. With a doctorate in philosophy from The Catholic University of America, his published writings revolve around the relation between religion and government.